ESPAÑOL ¡EN VIVO!

INSTRUCTIONAL SPANISH WORKBOOK
FOR GRADES 4-8

LEVEL 3

SARAH ROWAN

*Join our email list and receive free
lesson plans and special promotions!*

info@envivopublications.com
www.EnVivoPublications.com
360-383-7002

Español En Vivo Instructional Workbook Level 3 for Grades 4-8

Credits:
Author: Sarah Rowan
Cover Illustration: Mary Frances Brown
Maps: Jeremy Davies

¡Bienvenidos!

About the Author

Sarah Rowan is currently the director and lead instructor at Salud Spanish Programs in Bellingham, WA.

Sarah has taught in many different settings, ranging from the school classroom to programs offered at her own Spanish language school. Besides teaching, she has been creating curriculum for children and adults for over 26 years.

Sarah received her M.A. in Spanish Literature at the University of Louisville, and has lived and traveled in Latin America and Spain.

About Español ¡En Vivo! Instructional Workbook Level 3

Español ¡En Vivo! Level 3 is the third workbook in the En Vivo instructional workbook series, offering a simple and realistic approach to learning the Spanish language while encompassing interesting cultural elements to which students can relate.

There are 5 units, each one containing 5 progressive lessons, with dynamic spoken and written activities that allow students to practice in a fun and meaningful way. At the end of each unit, there is an *Enfoque de Carrera* in which students will read interviews with people of various professions around the country, highlighting the various uses and benefits of Spanish in their workplace.

Enjoy **ESPAÑOL EN VIVO Level 3**!

Sarah Rowan
En Vivo Publications
www.EnVivoPublications.com
360-383-7002

Join our email list and receive free lesson plans!
EnVivoPublications.com

¿Dónde se habla español?

Where is Spanish spoken?

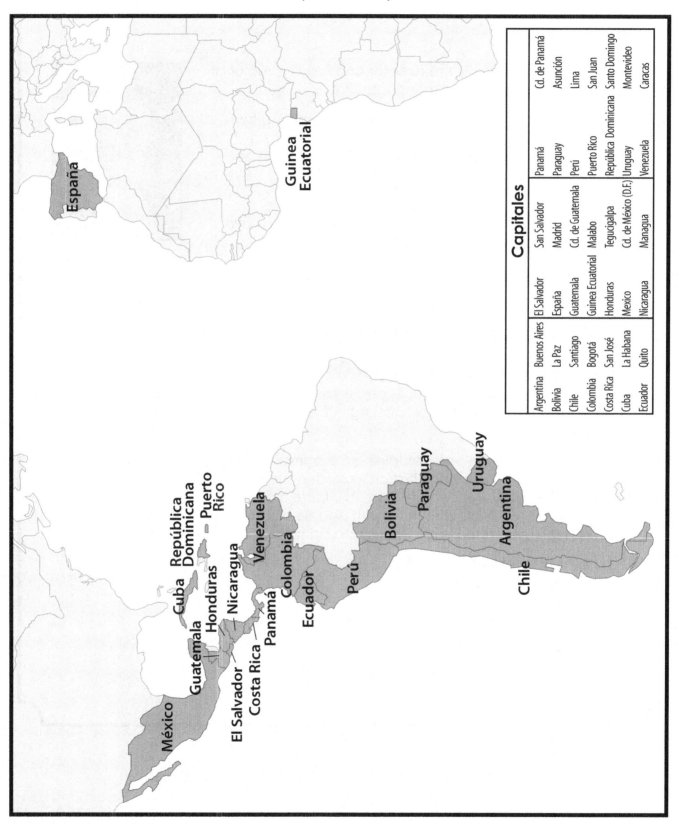

Capitales			
Argentina	Buenos Aires	El Salvador	San Salvador	Panamá	Cd. de Panamá
Bolivia	La Paz	España	Madrid	Paraguay	Asunción
Chile	Santiago	Guatemala	Cd. de Guatemala	Perú	Lima
Colombia	Bogotá	Guinea Ecuatorial	Malabo	Puerto Rico	San Juan
Costa Rica	San José	Honduras	Tegucigalpa	República Dominicana	Santo Domingo
Cuba	La Habana	México	Cd. de México (D.F.)	Uruguay	Montevideo
Ecuador	Quito	Nicaragua	Managua	Venezuela	Caracas

Índice / Table of Contents

PRONUNCIACIÓN

Letter	English sound		Examples
a	ah	f**a**ther	**mano** (hand), **cabeza** (head)
e	eh	m**e**t	**pez** (fish), **pelo** (hair)
i	ee	m**ee**t	**libro** (book), **gallina** (chicken)
o	oh	**o**pen	**oso** (bear), **mono** (monkey)
u	oo	sp**oo**n	**nublado** (cloudy), **azul** (blue)
h	--	*h is silent*	**helado** (ice cream), **hoja** (leaf)
j	h	**h**ot	**ajo** (garlic), **jamón** (ham)
ll	y	torti**ll**a	**silla** (chair), **estrella** (star)
ñ	ny	can**y**on	**España** (Spain), **araña** (spider)
rr	rr	*rr is "rolled"*	**perro** (dog), **gorra** (hat)
v	b	**b**at	**uva** (grape), **volcán** (volcano)
z*	ss	**s**at	**zanahoria** (carrot), **luz** (light)

* The "z" in Latin America sounds like an "s" while in Spain, it's pronounced with a "th" sound. This goes for "ci" and "ce" combinations, as well.

DIPTONGOS (Diphthongs)

A diphthong is a sound formed by the combination of two vowels. Try some of these! What do these words mean?

au ("ow")	**ai** ("ay")	**eu** ("eh-oo")	**ei** ("eh-ee")	**ie** ("ee-eh")	**ui** ("oo-ee")
auto	**ai**re	**Eu**ropa	r**ei**na	h**ie**lo	r**ui**do
j**au**la	b**ai**le	**eu**ro	ac**ei**te	n**ie**ve	c**ui**dado
fl**au**ta	v**ai**nilla	**Eu**genio	v**ei**nte	m**ie**l	b**ui**tre

UNIDAD 1

Las rutinas diarias

Daily Routines

❖ Lección 1: Diálogos (Dialogues)

In **En Vivo Level 1** and **Level 2**, you've practiced introducing yourself and greeting people. Here's a quick re-cap of the expressions:

Hola.	Hello.
Buenos días.	Good morning.
Buenas tardes.	Good afternoon.
Buenas noches.	Good night.
¿Cómo te llamas?	What is your name?
Me llamo...	My name is...
Mucho gusto.	Nice to meet you.
Igualmente.	Likewise.
¿Cómo estás? / ¿Qué tal?	How are you?
(Muy) bien.	(Very) well.
Regular. / Así así. / Más o menos.	So-so.
Mal.	Bad.
¿Y tú?	And you?
¿De dónde eres?	Where are you from?
Soy de...	I am from...
¿Cuál es tu número de teléfono?	What is your phone number?
Hasta luego. / Nos vemos.	See you later.
Adiós. / Chao.	Goodbye.

 PRACTICAR

1. Review the list of greetings above with your teacher and classmates, with brief spontaneous dialogues.

2. On the following page, you'll see a series of prompts that you will use to interview your classmates about various aspects of their lives.

   a. Write down the questions you will need to ask in the space provided.

   b. Then, conduct an interview with a classmate, recording his or her answer. For the first question, ask for the spelling of his or her name.

Entrevista

Fecha: _____

Pregunta:	Respuesta:

Nombre: _____   _____

Apellido(s): _____   _____

Dirección: _____   _____

Teléfono: _____   _____

Edad: _____   _____

Origen: _____   _____

Familia: _____   _____

Mascota(s): _____   _____

Escuela : _____   _____

Color favorito: _____   _____

Clase favorita: _____   _____

Pasatiempos: _____   _____

Personalidad: _____   _____

Notas: _____

_____

_____

¡Ojo!

You have learned how to ask lots of questions in Spanish, such as:

¿Cómo estás?	*How are you?*
¿Necesitas agua?	*Do you need water?*
¿Tienes hermanos?	*Do you have siblings?*

There are actually two ways of addressing someone in Spanish, an **informal way**, and a **formal way**. You have learned the **informal**, which is indicated by the verb form with an **'s'** at the end, as well as the subject pronoun **tú**, oftentimes implied and not stated.

The **formal way** of addressing someone is used when you don't know the person very well, or if you're talking to someone who is older. It's a way of showing respect. The verb form looks just like the one used with **él** and **ella**, and the accompanying subject pronoun is **usted**.

The questions above would look like this in the **formal**:

¿Cómo está usted?	*How are you?*
¿Necesita usted agua?	*Do you need water?*
¿Tiene usted hermanos?	*Do you have any siblings?*

Compare the following questions and statements below:

	Informal	Formal
Do you want to play?	¿**Quieres** jugar?	¿**Quiere** jugar usted?
Are you sad?	¿**Estás** triste?	¿**Está** usted triste?
You need to study.	**Necesitas** estudiar.	Usted **necesita** estudiar.
You are brave.	**Eres** valiente.	Usted **es** valiente.
Do you play the flute?	¿**Tocas** la flauta?	¿**Toca** usted la flauta?
You play tennis well.	**Juegas** bien al tenis.	Usted **juega bien** al tenis.

ESCRIBIR ——————————————————————

A. The interview on page 3 was probably conducted in the *informal*, with the informal verb forms. Convert these questions to the **formal**, based on what you learned on the previous page.

1. **Informal:** ¿Cómo te llamas?   **Formal:** ¿Cómo se llama usted?

2. **Informal:** ¿Dónde vives?   **Formal:** _____

3. **Informal:** ¿Cuántos años tienes?   **Formal:** _____

4. **Informal:** ¿De dónde eres?   **Formal:** _____

5. **Informal:** ¿Tienes hermanos?   **Formal:** _____

6. **Informal:** ¿Tienes mascotas?   **Formal:** _____

B. Given the following scenarios, write down the appropriate question.

1. *You're asking your 80 year old neighbor if she **has** sugar you could use.* **(tener)**

_____

2. *You're asking your friend if he **knows** what time the game is.* **(saber)**

_____

3. *You met a friend of your parents, and you ask where he **lives**.* **(vivir)**

_____

4. *You ask your teammate if she **is** ok after she falls down.* **(estar)**

_____

5. *You ask your teacher if she **wants** an apple.* **(querer)**

_____

❖ *Lección 2: Mi horario* (My schedule)

Las Asignaturas (Subjects)

el arte	art
las ciencias (naturales)	(natural) sciences
la educación física	physical education
la geografía	geography
la historia	history
la informática	computer science
la lengua extranjera	foreign language
la literatura	literature
las matemáticas	math
la música	music
la química	chemistry

¡Ojo!

You may have noticed that many of the subject names in Spanish are very similar looking to their English counterparts. These are called cognates. While this can help us recognize words, it can be a challenge to correctly pronounce the words, as we often mistakenly fall back on our English pronunciation of the words.

For example, look at the word **literatura**. We can tell that this is the Spanish word for *literature*, but let's remember the Spanish vowel pronunciation rules when saying this word: **lee-teh-rah-too-rah**.

🗣 PRACTICAR

1. a. First, without looking at your book, listen to your teacher say the school subjects out loud, and while repeating them, see if you can understand what they mean.

b. Now, repeat this exercise, but this time, look at the words while you repeat them after your teacher.

2. Read the following diologue out loud with a classmate. Read it a second time, replacing names and classes with actual ones.

¡Hola Sue! ¿Cómo estás?

Muy bien. ¿Y tú, Karen?

Bien, gracias. ¿Qué clases tienes?

Tengo matemáticas, ciencias y arte.

Yo tengo arte también. Me gusta mucho.

A mí también.

Bueno, ¡nos vemos en clase!

Muy bien. ¡Hasta pronto!

3. a. Pretend the class schedule below is your schedule. Your teacher will ask you when you have various classes. Follow this model:

> *Maestro(a):* **¿Cuándo tienes informática?**
> *Estudiante:* **Tengo informática los lunes a las dos.**

b. Then, your teacher will ask you if you like certain classes:

> *Maestro(a):* **¿Te gusta la clase de matemáticas?**
> *Estudiante:* **Sí, me gusta mucho.**

c. Finally, practice these same questions with a classmate, adding one more question:

> *Estudiante #1:* **¿Cuál es tu clase favorita?**
> *Estudiante #2:* **Mi clase favorita es arte.**

Mi horario

Hora	lunes	martes	miércoles	jueves	viernes
9:15-9:55	matemáticas	historia	educación física	español	arte
10:00-10:40	música	matemáticas	historia	música	literatura
10:45-11:25	arte	ciencias	matemáticas	historia	educación física
11:30-12:10	historia	geografía	ciencias	matemáticas	historia
12:15-12:45	A L M U E R Z O				
12:45-1:15	R E C R E O				
1:15-1:55	ciencias	español	literatura	ciencias	matemáticas
2:00-2:40	informática	literatura	arte	geografía	ciencias

✎ ESCRIBIR

A. Fill in the table below with your own class schedule, in Spanish.

Hora	lunes	martes	miércoles	jueves	viernes

B. Take turns with a classmate asking each other about days and times of classes, and which classes you like and dislike.

C. Answer the following questions, based on your class schedule.

1. ¿Cuál es tu clase favorita? _____

2. ¿Cuál es tu clase menos favorita? _____

3. ¿A qué hora es el almuerzo? _____

4. ¿Qué clases tienes todos los días? _____

5. ¿En qué clases tienes mucha tarea? _____

6. ¿Cuándo tienes matemáticas? _____

7. ¿Cuánto tiempo dura una clase típica? _____

8. ¿En qué clase(s) estás más cansado(a)? _____

9. ¿A qué hora empieza la primera clase? _____

10. ¿A qué hora termina la última clase? _____

D. ¿Qué necesitas? What do you need for the following classes? Follow the example below to complete the sentences. Include lunch!

un lápiz   un libro   una calculadora

un microscopio   un globo terráqueo   pinturas

tijeras   un cuaderno   música

Por ejemplo: Para **informática**, necesito **una computadora**.
For computer class, I need a computer.

1. Para _____, necesito _____.

2. Para _____, necesito _____.

3. Para _____, necesito _____.

4. Para _____, necesito _____.

5. Para _____, necesito _____.

6. Para _____, necesito _____.

7. Para _____, necesito _____.

8. Para _____, necesito _____.

❖ **Lección 3: Las profesiones**

(Professions)

Cuando sea mayor, quiero ser...

When I'm older, I want to be a...

abogado(a)	lawyer	**jardinero(a)**	gardener
actor/actriz	actor	**maestro(a), profesor(a)**	teacher
arqueólogo(a)	archaeologist		
artista	artist	**mecánico**	mechanic
astronauta	astronaut	**médico(a)**	doctor
bibliotecario(a)	librarian	**mesero(a), camarero(a)**	waiter/waitress
bombero(a)	firefighter		
carpintero(a)	carpenter	**músico**	musician
científico(a)	scientist	**peluquero(a)**	hair stylist/barber
cirujano(a)	surgeon	**piloto**	pilot
cocinero(a)	cook	**pintor(a)**	painter
contable	accountant	**plomero(a)**	plumber
dentista	dentist	**policía**	police officer
diseñador(a)	designer	**político**	politician
enfermero(a)	nurse	**programador(a)**	programmer
escritor(a)	writer	**secretario(a)**	secretary
fotógrafo(a)	photographer	**traductor(a)**	translator
ingeniero(a)	engineer	**veterinario(a)**	veterinarian

Nota: Some professions maintain the masculine form for females. Ask your teacher about them.

The article *un/una* is not included when identifying yourself or someone as a student or with a profession, except when an adjective is introduced.

Por ejemplo:
Ella es dentista.	*She's a dentist.*
Ella es una dentista buena.	*She's a good dentist.*
Soy estudiante.	*I am a student.*
Soy un estudiante fabuloso.	*I am a great student.*

 PRACTICAR

1. Practice saying the professions in Spanish, with the phrase, "Cuando sea mayor, quiero ser..." Remember, you don't need "un/una" before the word, but make sure you use the appropriate gender ending.

2. Choose a profession without telling anyone. Your classmates will ask you "sí" or "no" questions in order to guess what it is. Here are some possible questions. Add more questions in the space provided.

¿Es un trabajo peligroso?	¿Trabajas con animales?
¿Es un trabajo solitario?	¿Trabajas con medicina?
¿Es un trabajo al aire libre?	¿Trabajas con comida?
¿Es un trabajo técnico?	¿Trabajas con niños?

_____

_____

_____

_____

_____

_____

3. You are interviewing someone for a job. Decide what position *(puesto)* you'd like to interview someone for, and then fill out the following chart. Then, conduct the interview with at least one classmate.

Puesto: _____   **Fecha:** _____
     (policía, dentista, artista, etc.)

Nombre: _____   **Teléfono:** _____
     (de la persona entrevistada)

Descripción del puesto:

Este puesto de _____ requiere una persona _____ y
                    (puesto)   *(adjetivo)*

_____ que le gusta estar con _____. No es
     (adjetivo)   *(personas, niños, animales, etc.)*

necesario ser _____ ni _____. Nunca va a estar con
                    (adjetivo)   *(adjetivo)*

_____. Las horas son _____. Se prefiere experiencia
(personas, niños, animales, etc.)   *(flexibles, fijas, largas, etc.)*

de _____ años con _____.
        (años)   *(música, animales, fotografía, etc.)*

Preguntas:

1. ¿Prefiere usted un horario flexible o fijo?

2. ¿Prefiere estar usted con animales o con la computadora?

3. ¿Puede usted ver sangre sin problemas?

4. ¿Es usted una persona sociable?

5. ¿Le gusta explorar?

6. ¿Le gustaría ser el/la presidente(a)?

7. ¿Toca usted un instrumento?

8. ¿Prefiere trabajar usted con niños?

9. _____

10. _____

Notas: _____

_____

_____

✏ ESCRIBIR

A. Match the professions with the activities with which they are commonly associated. Look up any words you do not know in the second column.

1. un fotógrafo ____   a. escribe libros
2. una bibliotecaria ____   b. organiza libros
3. un bombero ____   c. construye casas
4. una escritora ____   d. toca la guitarra
5. un enfermero ____   e. explora el espacio exterior
6. una ingeniera ____   f. diseña edificios y puentes
7. un carpintero ____   g. trabaja con asuntos legales
8. una abogada ____   h. saca fotos
9. un músico ____   i. apaga incendios
10. una astronauta ____   j. cuida a la gente enferma

B. Complete the following sentences with the appropriate profession.

1. Una _____ hace comidas muy buenas para mucha gente.

2. El _____ representa a otras personas en asuntos legales.

3. Cuando agua sale de los tubos, llamamos al _____.

4. En el hospital hay médicos y _____.

5. Si mi perro está enfermo, lo llevo a la _____.

6. Mi jardín es un desastre total. Voy a llamar a mi _____.

7. El servicio en este restaurante es bueno. Tienen buenos _____.

8. Con más violencia en las calles, necesitamos más _____.

9. Mi pelo está largo. Voy a la _____ esta semana.

10. Un buen _____ hace muebles de madera muy bonitos.

C. 1. First go over the adjectives below with your teacher. Do you recognize some of them? Can you think of other adjectives that are commonly associated to the professions listed on page 11?

paciente	inteligente	aventurero(a)	cariñoso(a)
creativo(a)	fuerte	diplomático(a)	curioso(a)
informado(a)	justo(a)	imaginativo(a)	meticuloso(a)
dramático(a)	sociable	extrovertido	introvertido
estudioso(a)	estable	simpático(a)	preciso(a)
tranquilo(a)	confiable	hábil con las manos	valiente

2. Think of 3 professions that interest you, and state why you think you would be good in that field.

Por ejemplo: Quiero ser arqueóloga porque soy aventurera.

1. Quiero ser _____, porque soy _____.

2. Quiero ser _____, porque soy _____.

3. Quiero ser _____, porque soy _____.

3. Now, think of 3 professions that do not interest you, and state why you think you would not be good in that field.

Por ejemplo: No quiero ser maestro porque no soy justo.

1. No quiero ser _____, porque (no) soy _____.

2. No quiero ser _____, porque (no) soy _____.

3. No quiero ser _____, porque (no) soy _____.

❖ **Lección 4: Los quehaceres** (Chores)

Miguel **lava la ropa**.

Raúl **friega el suelo**.

Eva **plancha** la camisa.

Pedro **saca la basura**.

Cruz **pasa la aspiradora**.

Linda **hace la cama**.

Mateo **lava los platos**.

Larry **corta el césped**.

Juanito **barre el suelo**.

barrer el suelo	*to sweep the floor*
cortar el césped/el pasto	*to mow the lawn*
fregar	*to mop/to scrub/to wash*
hacer la cama	*to make the bed*
lavar los platos	*to wash the dishes*
lavar la ropa	*to wash the clothes*
limpiar	*to clean*
pasar la aspiradora	*to vacuum*
planchar	*to iron*
poner la mesa	*to set the table*
recoger/quitar la mesa	*to clear the table*
regar las plantas	*to water the plants*
sacar la basura	*to take out the garbage*

 PRACTICAR

1. Repeat the sentences on the previous page after your teacher, acting them out as you do so.

2. Your teacher will now ask you who does the following chores, and you will respond in complete sentences.
   Por ejemplo: ¿Quién **corta** el césped?   — Larry **corta** el césped.

3. With a partner, continue the same activity, taking turns asking and answering the questions.

4. With the same partner, ask whether or not he or she typically does these chores.
   Por ejemplo: ¿**Sacas** la basura?   — Sí, **saco** la basura.

¡Ojo!

You have learned the informal **tú** and formal **usted** ways of addressing someone in Spanish, but what if you are talking to more than one person, as in, "Do you all have money?" or "What do you all want to do?"

Just like in the singular, there is an informal and a formal way to address "you all": **vosotros(as)** (informal) and **ustedes** (formal).

The **vosotros** verb form in the present tense is formed like this:

-ar ending verbs → **áis**	**Ejemplo:** Habl**áis**...	*You all talk...*
-er ending verbs → **éis**	**Ejemplo:** Com**éis**...	*You all eat...*
-ir ending verbs → **ís**	**Ejemplo:** Viv**ís**...	*You all live...*

The **ustedes** verb form in the present tense is the same as the **ellos** and **ellas**. **Por ejemplo:** Ustedes hablan español. *You all speak Spanish.*

The catch is, they use both of these forms in Spain while they only use the formal **ustedes** in Latin America, regardless of the group being addressed.

Por ejemplo:

Vosotros tenéis un gato. *You all have a cat.* **(informal in Spain)**

Ustedes tienen un gato. *You all have a cat.* **(formal in Spain)**
(formal and informal in L.A.)

5. In groups of 3-4 students, take turns asking each other the questions below. Mark with an **X** all the possible scenarios that apply to the verb form used in each of the questions.

When responding, one person can answer for the group in the **nosotros(as)** form, or each person can answer individually with the **yo** form.

	En España con amigos	En España con maestros	En México con amigos o maestros
1. ¿Tenéis hambre?			
2. ¿Dónde viven ustedes?			
3. ¿Habláis alemán?			
4. ¿Vivís en España?			
5. ¿Planchan ustedes?			

¡Ojo! You know how to express what one needs or needs to do with the verb *necesitar*, as in: **Marta necesita dormir.** *(Marta needs to sleep.)*

Similarly, we can talk about what we *"have to do"* with the following expression with *tener*:

yo	**tengo**				
tú	**tienes**				
él, ella, usted	**tiene**	+	QUE	+	INFINITIVE
nosotros(as)	**tenemos**				
vosotros(as)	**tenéis**				
ellos, ellas, ustedes	**tienen**				

Por ejemplo:

Tengo que limpiar el baño.   *I have to clean the bathroom.*
Ustedes **tienen que hacer** la cama.   *You all have to make the bed.*
Tenemos que barrer el suelo.   *We have to sweep the floor.*
Mis amigos **tienen que lavar** los platos.   *My friends have to wash the dishes.*
Tienes que planchar la ropa.   *You have to iron the clothes.*

6. In pairs, take turns asking what the other person has to do tonight *(esta noche)*, tomorrow *(mañana)* and this weekend *(este fin de semana)*. Record your own responses to the questions in the blanks provided.

1. ¿Qué tienes que hacer esta noche?

   – *Tengo que* _____

2. ¿Qué tienes que hacer mañana?

   – _____

3. ¿Qué tienes que hacer este fin de semana?

   – _____

✏️ ESCRIBIR

A. Complete the following table, placing an '**X**' indicating how frequently you do the following chores.

	Todos los días	Una vez a la semana	De vez en cuando	Nunca
1. ¿Sacas la basura?				
2. ¿Haces la cama?				
3. ¿Cortas el césped?				
4. ¿Limpias el baño?				
5. ¿Pasas la aspiradora?				
6. ¿Lavas los platos?				
7. ¿Planchas la ropa?				
8. ¿Lavas la ropa?				
9. ¿Barres el suelo?				
10. ¿Pones la mesa?				

B. Pick 6 chores from above and write out your responses in complete sentences. **Por ejemplo:** Lavo los platos todos los días.

1. _____

2. _____

3. _____

4. _____

5. _____

6. _____

C. Compare your chores with 2-3 other classmates out loud, noting your similarities and differences.

> **Por ejemplo:** Sue no tiene que hacer la cama nunca, y
> yo tengo que hacer la cama todos los días.

D. State what the following people *have to do* in the given situations, using **tener + que + infinitive**.

1. Hay muchos platos y comida en la mesa.

   Juanito _____ .

2. La hierba está muy larga.

   Marta _____ .

3. La bañera *(bathtub)* está muy sucia.

   Yo _____ .

4. Los abuelos van a visitar mañana y quieren ver toda la casa.

   Toda la familia _____ .

5. Las plantas tienen mucha sed.

   Eduardo _____ .

6. Hay mucha basura en la cocina después de la fiesta.

   Nosotros _____ .

7. Los platos están sucios.

   Marta y Diego _____ .

8. Hay mucho pelo del perro en el suelo.

   Berta _____ .

9. No tienes ropa limpia.

   Yo _____ .

10. La ropa está arrugada *(wrinkled)*.

    José _____ .

❖ **Lección 5: Repaso** *(Review)*

A. Match the Spanish words with the English counterparts.

1. horario	____		a.	cleans
2. barre	____		b.	bed
3. césped	____		c.	schedule
4. plancha	____		d.	hair stylist/barber
5. química	____		e.	plumber
6. geografía	____		f.	sweeps
7. cocinero(a)	____		g.	surgeon
8. escritor(a)	____		h.	washes
9. basura	____		i.	teacher
10. jardinero(a)	____		j.	lawn
11. maestro(a)	____		k.	vacuum cleaner
12. cirujano(a)	____		l.	irons
13. literatura	____		m.	floor
14. limpia	____		n.	chemistry
15. cama	____		o.	literature
16. lava	____		p.	geography
17. suelo	____		q.	gardener
18. plomero(a)	____		r.	cook/chef
19. peluquero(a)	____		s.	garbage
20. aspiradora	____		t.	writer

B. Walk around the room pretending like you don't know anyone. Greet and collect the following information in Spanish from at least 3 classmates:

- Names and spelling
- How they are doing
- Age
- Profession(s) of interest
- Personality qualities
- Household chores

Enfoque de Carrera

Cocinera
30 años
Nashville, TN

Susan Jones

Laura: Hola Susan. Gracias por hablar conmigo. ¿Puede decirme usted *desde cuando trabaja* como cocinera?

Susan: Hola Laura. Sí, claro, trabajo como cocinera desde hace 20 años, pero en este restaurante sólo 5 años.

Laura: ¿Qué es lo que más le gusta de su trabajo?

Susan: Uy, esto es difícil porque me gustan muchos aspectos de mi trabajo, pero si tengo que decir lo que más me gusta es la creatividad que me *brinda* mi trabajo a la hora de preparar los platos diferentes.

Laura: ¿Qué es lo que menos le gusta de su trabajo?

Susan: Sin duda, la jornada laboral que se hace muy larga. Nunca sé cuando voy a terminar por la noche, y a veces estoy muy cansada.

Laura: ¿Tiene usted la oportunidad de usar su español durante el trabajo?

Susan: Sí, todas las semanas. Nuestro *vendedor* principal de verduras, frutas y pan sólo habla español. Aunque mi español no es perfecto, hablo lo suficiente para comunicarme con él. *Además*, cuando tenemos clientes *hispanohablantes*, siempre salgo *un ratito* para saludarles y explicarles el menú.

Laura: ¿Tiene planes para el *futuro cercano*?

Susan: Bueno, no sé cuando, pero mi sueño es abrir mi propio restaurante. ¡Ya tengo un nombre... La Susana!

Laura: ¿Cuál es su palabra favorita en español?

Susan: *Zanahoria* es mi palabra favorita en español, ¡y es mi verdura favorita!

VOCABULARIO:

desde cuando trabaja usted - how long have you been working   ***brinda*** - offers
jornada laboral - work day   ***vendedor*** - vendor   ***un ratito*** - a little while
hispanohablantes-Spanish-speaking   ***además***-additionally   ***futuro cercano***-near future

Enfoque de Carrera ◆ Discusión

A. Lee la entrevista en la página anterior en voz alta.

B. Contesta las preguntas sobre la entrevista.

1. ¿A qué se dedica Susan Jones? _____

2. ¿Desde cuándo trabaja como cocinera? _____

3. ¿De dónde es? _____

4. ¿Cuántos años tiene? _____

5. ¿Qué es lo que más le gusta de su trabajo? _____

6. ¿Qué es lo que menos le gusta? _____

7. ¿Habla español en su trabajo? _____

8. ¿Qué planes tiene para el futuro?_____

9. ¿Cuál es su palabra favorita en español? _____

◆ ◆ ◆

C. Ahora responde a las preguntas personales sobre este tema.

1. ¿Te gusta cocinar? _____

2. ¿A veces preparas la cena? _____

3. ¿Qué plato te gusta hacer? _____

4. ¿Te gustaría ser cocinero(a) algún día? _____

5. ¿Por qué sería útil saber español en esta carrera? _____

◆ ◆ ◆

D. Comparte tus respuestas con la clase.

UNIDAD

Las celebraciones y excursiones

Celebrations and Outings

❖ Lección 1: ¡Fiesta! *(Party!)*

Felicidades

los globos

el pastel

el regalo

el invitado

abrir	to open	el cumpleaños	birthday
cantar	to sing	la fiesta (sorpresa)	(surprise) party
celebrar	to celebrate	los globos	balloons
cumplir (años)	to turn (an age)	el pastel/la tarta	cake
gritar	to shout/scream	las velas	candles
pasar(lo) bien	to have a good time	los invitados	guests
pedir un deseo	to make a wish	el regalo	gift
soplar las velas	to blow out candles		

🗣 PRACTICAR

1. Read along as your teacher reads the following text out loud, and then practice with a classmate. See what you can piece together with only the vocabulary list above. Don't worry if you can't understand everything. You're not supposed to yet!

"Ayer **fui**[1] a una fiesta sorpresa para Ana. Ella **cumplió**[2] 9 años. Todos los invitados **gritaron**[3] "FELIZ CUMPLEAÑOS" y le **cantamos**[4] cuando ella **entró**[5]. Ella **sopló**[6] las velas, **comimos**[7] pastel y **escuchamos**[8] música. Después, Ana **abrió**[9] unos regalos. ¡Todos lo **pasamos**[10] muy bien!

Write the infintives of the verbs (in bold) in the story above. Feel free to guess or leave it blank until you study the next page.

1. _____   6. _____

2. _____   7. _____

3. _____   8. _____

4. _____   9. _____

5. _____   10. _____

You may have noted that the story on the previous page was told in the past tense, with verbs with different endings. This is the preterite tense, one of the two past tenses in Spanish, used for completed actions in the past.

One of the verbs, **IR** (to go), looks very different from the infinitive, but it happens to be a very commonly used verb in the preterite tense:

¡Ojo!

<u>ir</u> (to go)

yo	**fui**	*I went*
tú	**fuiste**	*you went (informal)*
él, ella, usted	**fue**	*he/she/you (formal) went*
nosotros(as)	**fuimos**	*we went*
vosotros(as)	**fuisteis**	*you all went (inf.-Spain)*
ellos, ellas, ustedes	**fueron**	*they went, you all went (f.)*

The following verb is an example of a <u>**regular -ar ending verb**</u> in the past:

<u>grit**ar**</u> (to scream)

yo	**grit<u>é</u>**	*I screamed*
tú	**grit<u>aste</u>**	*you screamed (informal)*
él, ella, usted	**grit<u>ó</u>**	*he/she/you (formal) screamed*
nosotros(as)	**grit<u>amos</u>**	*we screamed*
vosotros(as)	**grit<u>asteis</u>**	*you all screamed (inf.-Spain)*
ellos, ellas, ustedes	**grit<u>aron</u>**	*they screamed, you all screamed (f.)*

The following verb is an example of a <u>**regular -er and -ir ending verb**</u> in the past:

<u>com**er**</u> (to eat)

yo	**com<u>í</u>**	*I ate*
tú	**com<u>iste</u>**	*you ate (informal)*
él, ella, usted	**com<u>ió</u>**	*he/she/you (formal) ate*
nosotros(as)	**com<u>imos</u>**	*we ate*
vosotros(as)	**com<u>isteis</u>**	*you all ate (inf.-Spain)*
ellos, ellas, ustedes	**com<u>ieron</u>**	*they ate, you all ate (f.)*

2. In pairs, take turns asking each other when the last time he or she did the following things. Use the example as a model. The following phrases may be useful:

> **ayer** - yesterday   **anoche** - last night   **hace 3 días** - 3 days ago
> **el mes pasado** - last month   **la semana pasada** - last week

Por ejemplo:

¿Cuándo fue la última vez que dormiste 12 horas?
When was the last time you slept 12 hours?

— Dormí 12 horas la semana pasada.
I slept 12 hours last week.

¿Cuándo fue la última vez que...

1. ... _____ (comer) pastel?

2. ... _____ (abrir) un regalo?

3. ... _____ (cantar) una canción entera?

4. ... _____ (ir) a la playa?

5. ... _____ (limpiar) tu cuarto?

6. ... _____ (cocinar) para la familia?

7. ... _____ (lavar) los platos?

8. ... _____ (subir) un árbol?

3. Your teacher now will ask you when the last time your partner did these things. See if you can remember the answer!

Por ejemplo: ¿Cuándo fue la última vez que Jane comió pastel?
— Jane comió pastel el jueves pasado.

✏️ ESCRIBIR

A. Fill in the blank with the appropriate word from the word bank, making any necessary changes. Note: You won't need to repeat the article.

las velas   el regalo   los invitados
el pastel   la fiesta   los globos

1. Ana cumplió 9 años, entonces hay nueve _____ en el pastel.

2. Ella prefiere un _____ de fresa.

3. Todos los _____ gritaron "¡FELIZ CUMPLEAÑOS!".

4. Los _____ son grandes y de muchos colores.

5. Ayer fuimos a una_____ sorpresa para Ana.

6. Después de comer pastel, Ana abrió los _____ .

B. Translate the following sentences into the preterite tense.

1. They went to a surpise party yesterday.

_____

2. Ana ate a lot of cake.

_____

3. Did you listen to the music?

_____

4. My dad turned 45 on Tuesday.

_____

5. We celebrated his birthday on Saturday.

_____

6. I sang happy birthday.

_____

C. In pairs, using the verbs **comer**, **abrir**, and **gritar**, take turns quizzing each other, by stating a subject and a verb while the other conjugates the verb accordingly, and then states what it means in English.

Por ejemplo:

Compañero(a) #1:   *ella   gritar*
Compañero(a) #2:   Ella gritó.   *She screamed.*

D. Complete the following crossword puzzle with the Spanish words for each of the clues in English.

CRUCIGRAMA (¡Fiesta!)

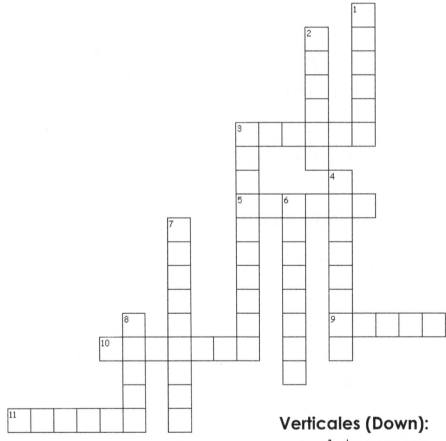

Horizontales (Across):
3. to sing
5. cake
9. to open
10. gifts
11. balloons

Verticales (Down):
1. to scream
2. party
3. birthday
4. to celebrate
6. surprise
7. guests
8. candles

❖ *Lección 2: Las excursiones* (Outings)

¿Qué hiciste el fin de semana pasado?
What did you do last weekend?

— Fui...
I went...

...a la ciudad.

...a las montañas.

...a la costa.

...al campo.

¡Ojo!

The common question found on the previous page contains the verb **hiciste** which is the irregular preterite tense of the verb **hacer** (to do/make).

yo	**hice**	I did / made
tú	**hiciste**	you did / made (inf.)
él, ella, usted	**hizo**	he, she, you (f.) did / made
nosotros(as)	**hicimos**	we did / made
vosotros(as)	**hicisteis**	you all (inf.-Spain) did / made
ellos, ellas, ustedes	**hicieron**	they, you all (f.) did / made

la costa

nadar	*to swim*
tomar el sol	*to sunbathe*
jugar en la playa	*to play on beach*
navegar	*to sail*
volar una cometa	*to fly a kite*

las montañas

acampar	*to camp*
caminar	*to walk, hike*
escalar	*to climb*
esquiar	*to ski*
hacer snowboard	*to snowboard*

el campo

ir de pícnic	*to picnic*
ir de caza	*to hunt*
ir de pesca	*to fish*
ir en canoa	*to canoe*
montar a caballo	*to horseback ride*

la ciudad

ir...	*to go...*
...al museo	*...to the museum*
...al teatro	*...to the theater*
...a un concierto	*...to a concert*
salir a comer/cenar	*to go out to eat*

 **PRACTICAR** ────────────────────────────

1. Play charades in groups designated by your teacher using the verbs on the previous page.

    a. First round, the person(s) guessing will use the infinitive of the verb, along with the verb **¿Quieres...?** (Do you want...?).

        Por ejemplo:

        ¿Quieres **tomar el sol**?
               — ¡Sí, quiero tomar el sol!

    b. Second round, the person(s) guessing will use the preterite tense of the verb.

        Por ejemplo:

        ¿**Escalaste**?
             — ¡Sí, **escalé**!

2. In pairs, ask your partner where he/she went and what he/she did last summer (**el verano pasado**).

        Por ejemplo:

        ¿A dónde fuiste el verano pasado?
             — El verano pasado, fui a la costa.

        ¿Qué hiciste?
             — **Nadé**, **jugué** en la playa y **volé** una cometa.

3. In small groups, take turns asking about what your classmates like and dislike to do. If you don't know how to do something, you say:
No sé + infivitve. (I don't know how to + infinitive)

Por ejemplo:

¿Te gusta esquiar o hacer snowboard? *Do you like to ski or snowboard?*
   — Me gusta esquiar. *I like to ski.*

¿Te gusta navegar? *Do you like to sail?*
   — No sé navegar. *I don't know how to sail.*

¿Te gusta ir de pesca? *Do you like to fish?*
   — No, no me gusta ir de pesca. *No, I don't like to fish.*

 ESCRIBIR ─────────────────────────

A. Write down what the following people did last weekend. Begin each sentence with ***El fin de semana pasado...*** (Last weekend...)

Gloria

Pedro y Paco

Andrea

Sue y Bob

Marta

Raúl

1. _____

2. _____

3. _____

4. _____

5. _____

6. _____

B. ¿Qué necesitas? What do you need when you go to the mountains? What about the coast, the city or the country? Complete the following sentences, choosing from the items in the box. Add other items that you think may be useful.

un traje de baño   el dinero   una mochila

las botas   las gafas de sol   una canoa

una cámara   el protector solar   una tienda de campaña

Por ejemplo:

Para **ir a las montañas**, necesito **una tienda de campaña**.
To go to the mountains, I need a tent.

1. Para _____, necesito _____

_____.

2. Para _____, necesito _____

_____.

3. Para _____, necesito _____

_____.

4. Para _____, necesito _____

_____.

❖ *Lección 3: ¡Vamos de vacaciones!*
(Let's go on vacation!)

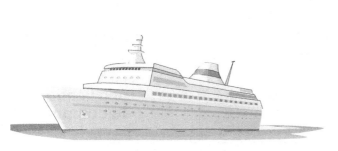

en crucero

en la playa

Vacaciones

culturales

de aventura

el alpinismo	*mountaineering*	**las vacaciones...**	
el buceo	*scuba diving*	**...culturales**	*cultural vacation*
el parque de atracciones	*amusement park*	**...de aventura**	*adventure vacation*
la reunión familiar	*family reunion*	**...en crucero**	*cruise vacation*
		...en la playa	*beach vacation*
esquiar	*to ski*	**...en el extranjero**	*vacation abroad*
sacar fotos	*to take photos*	**...en casa**	*staycation*
viajar	*to travel*		

The **conditional tense** (*the "would" tense*) is useful when you don't have a set plan but you'd like to state what you **would** do. Notice how the unique set of endings are at the **end** of the infinitive:

	viajar	
Yo	viajar**ía**	*I would travel*
Tú	viajar**ías**	*You (informal) would travel*
Él, Ella, Usted	viajar**ía**	*He/She/You (formal) would travel*
Nosotros(as)	viajar**íamos**	*We would travel*
Vosotros(as)	viajar**íais**	*You all (inf.) would travel*
Ellos, Ellas, Uds.	viajar**ían**	*They/You all (f.) would travel*

If it's an irregular verb in the conditional (there are 12 of them), you place the same conditional ending right after the irregular base. Here are 3 common irregular verbs in the conditional:

	hacer	**decir**	**tener**
Yo	har**ía**	dir**ía**	tendr**ía**
Tú	har**ías**	dir**ías**	tendr**ías**
Él, Ella, Usted	har**ía**	dir**ía**	tendr**ía**
Nosotros(as)	har**íamos**	dir**íamos**	tendr**íamos**
Vosotros(as)	har**íais**	dir**íais**	tendr**íais**
Ellos, Ellas, Uds.	har**ían**	dir**ían**	tendr**ían**

 PRACTICAR

1. In pairs, discuss with your partner what your ideal trip *(tu viaje ideal)* would entail. Include the following:

- ¿Qué tipo de viaje sería?   Mi viaje ideal sería (would be) _____.
- ¿A dónde irías?   Iría a (I would go) _____.
- ¿Qué harías?   _____. (what you would do)
- ¿Cómo viajarías?   Viajaría en _____. (tren, avión, etc.)
- ¿Con quién irías?   Iría con _____. (amigos, padres, etc.)
- ¿Qué necesitarías?   Necesitaría _____.

_____

_____

_____

_____

_____

_____

Mi viaje ideal

(Dibuja una escena de tu viaje ideal)

2. **Planificador de vacaciones.** In groups, you will create a 1-week vacation plan with various options for the rest of your class, according to the vacation type assigned by your teacher:

- **Crucero**   • **Aventura**   • **Cultural**   • **Playa**

a. Tipo de vacaciones: _____

b. Lugar(es) de vacaciones: _____

c. Actividad(es) principal(es): _____

d. Ropa/cosas necesarias: _____

e. Costo del viaje: _____

f. Plan de vacaciones:
   (Escribe las actividades en los cuadros)

	lunes	martes	miércoles	jueves	viernes	sábado	domingo
Por la mañana							
Por la tarde							
Por la noche							

g. All groups will present their vacation plans, and then the class will vote on the vacation they would like to take.

 **ESCRIBIR**

A. Fill in the following table with specific activities according to the trip category and type of activity. Place an **'X'** in the box if you can't think of an activity that corresponds with the category.

	Activo/ejercicio	Interesante/educativo	Relajante/social
Aventura			
Cultural			
Crucero			
Playa			

B. Answer the following questions about your trip preferences and experiences in Spanish.

1. Cuando estás de viaje, ¿prefieres estar activo(a) o inactivo(a)?

   _____

2. ¿Viajaste alguna vez en el extranjero *(abroad)*?

   _____

3. ¿Para ti, es divertida *(fun)* o aburrida *(boring)* una reunion familiar?

   _____

4. ¿Cuál fue el viaje más peligroso que hiciste en tu vida?

   _____

5. ¿Cuál fue el viaje más relajante que hiciste en tu vida?

   _____

6. ¿Cuál fue el viaje más educativo que hiciste en tu vida?

   _____

C. Complete the following sentences with the correct form of the verb in the **CONDITIONAL** tense. Note: Verbs with an asterisk (*) are irregular.

1. Mis amigos _____ (esquiar) hoy, pero están enfermos.

2. Tú _____ (hacer*) la tarea, pero no tienes el libro.

3. Ella _____ (llevar) su camisa nueva pero está sucia.

4. Yo _____ (comprar) una casa en las montañas pero no me gusta la nieve.

5. Nosotros _____ (ir) a España pero no tenemos dinero.

6. Vosotros _____ (comer) un burrito pero no tenéis hambre.

7. Usted _____ (decir*) la verdad pero tiene miedo.

8. Ellos _____ (tener*) miedo pero la luz está encendida.

D. ¿Qué harías? Use the **CONDITIONAL** tense to state what you would do in the following situations.

1. Estás enfermo(a) después de comer ostras.

_____

2. Un amigo te pide (asks you for) dinero.

_____

3. Tu maestra se cae (falls) al suelo.

_____

4. Pierdes tu pasaporte en Argentina.

_____

5. Un dinosaurio está en tu habitación.

_____

❖ *Lección 4: ¿Cómo vamos?*
(How are we getting there?)

You learned how to talk about trips, outings and celebrations. Now, you're going to learn vocabulary and phrases associated with transportation.

Vamos en...
We're going by...

...coche    ...bicicleta

...avión    ...barco

...tren    ...autobús

el autobús/bus	*bus*	**la moto(cicleta)**	*motorcycle*
el avión	*airplane*	**el taxi**	*taxi*
el barco	*ship, boat*	**el tren**	*train*
la bici(cleta)	*bicycle (bike)*	**caminar**	*to walk*
el coche/el carro	*car*	**conducir/manejar**	*to drive*
el helicóptero	*helicopter*	**ir en...**	*to go by...*
el metro	*subway*	**ir a pie**	*to go on foot*

¡Ojo!

There are many different terms for the word "car" and "bus" in Spanish, depending on the country. Here are some of them:

	<u>Car</u>	<u>Bus</u>
Argentina:	**auto**	**colectivo**
Cuba:	**máquina**	**guagua**
Mexico:	**carro**	**camión**
Spain:	**coche**	**autobús**

🗣 PRACTICAR

1. In pairs, take turns asking each other how you get to certain places.

Por ejemplo: ¿Cómo vas **a la escuela**? — Voy en bicicleta.

¿Cómo vas...

a. ...**al centro comercial?** – _____

b. ...**a casa de tu amigo(a)?** – _____

c. ...**a una isla pequeña?** – _____

d. ...**a las montañas?** – _____

e. ...**a otro estado?** – _____

f. ..._____**?** – _____

2. Now, ask each other when the last time was that he or she went by car, bus, boat, etc. These expressions may be useful when responding:

anoche   **ayer**   **la semana pasada**   **el mes pasado**   **hace...**

Por ejemplo: ¿Cuándo fue la última vez que fuiste en avión?
— Fui a visitar a mi abuela en avión el mes pasado.

a. en barco	d. en bus	g. en taxi
b. en tren	e. en avión	h. en metro
c. en bici	f. a pie	i. en coche

3. In pairs, follow the flowchart below, and work your way through the conversation following the different paths. Repeat the activity until you've explored several options.

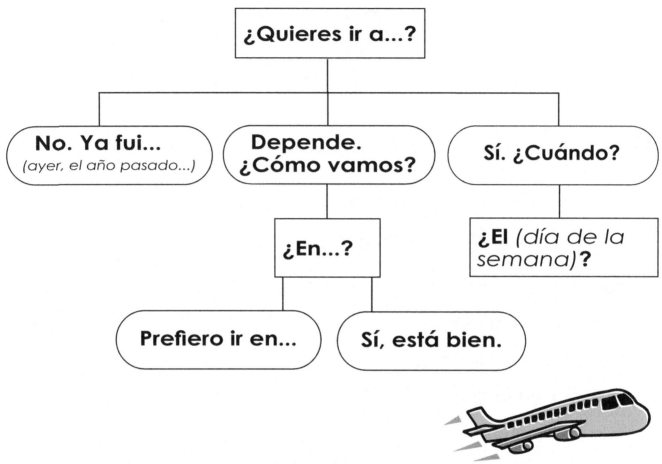

4. In pairs, ask each other the following questions.

1. ¿Puedes leer en el coche cuando estás de viaje?

2. ¿Tienes miedo en un avión si hay una tormenta u otra turbulencia?

3. ¿Eres capaz de dormir mientras viajas en coche? ¿En avión?, etc.

4. ¿Te llevas muchas cosas cuando viajas?

5. ¿Pasaste una vez más de un día en un barco?

ESCRIBIR ────────────────────────────────

A. In the following table, indicate with an '**X**' the means of transportation that have the following advantages. Discuss why, as well as the opposites of these adjectives.

Viajar en...	es divertido	es barato	es cómodo	es rápido
coche				
avión				
bicicleta				
tren				
barco				

B. Match the means of transportation with the most logical situation.

1. Voy en bicicleta. ___   a. Quiero flexibilidad total.

2. Voy en tren. ___   b. Me gusta caminar.

3. Voy en avión. ___   c. No tengo prisa y me gusta el mar.

4. Voy en barco. ___   d. Me gusta el acceso fácil y el ejercicio.

5. Voy en coche. ___   e. Vivo en la ciudad y no tengo coche.

6. Voy en metro. ___   f. Tengo prisa y mi destino queda lejos.

7. Voy a pie. ___   g. Es barato y puedo dormir en la ruta.

C. Answer the following questions about your travel preferences and experiences in Spanish.

1. ¿Qué medio de transporte prefieres? ¿Por qué?

   _____

2. ¿Viajaste alguna vez en avión por más de 3 horas?

   _____

3. ¿Cuál fue la distancia más larga que viajaste en bicicleta?

   _____

4. ¿Te mareas fácilmente en coche? ...en avión? ...en barco?

   _____

❖ *Lección 5: El Repaso (Review)*

A. Match the Spanish words with the English counterparts.

1. avión	____	a.	guest	
2. buceo	____	b.	beach	
3. crucero	____	c.	airplane	
4. vela	____	d.	party	
5. coche	____	e.	mountaineering	
6. ciudad	____	f.	scuba diving	
7. a pie	____	g.	boat	
8. aventura	____	h.	mountain	
9. tren	____	i.	cruise	
10. barco	____	j.	country, farmland	
11. invitado(a)	____	k.	vacation	
12. fiesta	____	l.	candle	
13. campo	____	m.	train	
14. pastel	____	n.	gift	
15. cumpleaños	____	o.	car	
16. regalo	____	p.	cake	
17. vacaciones	____	q.	birthday	
18. montaña	____	r.	city	
19. alpanismo	____	s.	adventure	
20. playa	____	t.	on foot	

B. Walk around the room pretending like you don't know anyone, and have short conversations with at least 3 people. Include:

- Greet each other
- Ask what he/she did last weekend (*el fin de semana pasado*)
- Ask what he/she ate yesterday (*use the preterite tense*)
- Ask where he/she went last week (*use the preterite tense*)
- Ask what he/she **would do** with $50 (*use the conditional tense*)
- Ask where he/she wants to go on vacation
- Say goodbye.

Enfoque de Carrera

Bombero
paracaidista
32 años
San Diego, CA

Ricky Mason

Laura: Hola Ricky. Usted es bombero paracaidista. ¿Está usted loco?

Ricky: Jajaja, la verdad, Laura, es que sí, estoy un poco loco. Pero resulta que ser bombero coincidió con mi pasatiempo de paracaidismo de modo muy beneficioso.

Laura: ¿Qué es lo que más le gusta de su trabajo?

Ricky: Lo que más me gusta de mi trabajo es la pura *descarga de adrenalina* que recibo cuando estoy *de turno*.

Laura: Me imagino. ¿Qué es lo que menos le gusta de su trabajo?

Ricky: Tengo que estar *de guardia* 24 horas al día 7 días a la semana durante la temporada de incendios. Un año trabajé 21 días consecutivos. Se me hace difícil hacer planes o ir de vacaciones con mi familia.

Laura: ¿Qué estudió usted?

Ricky: Estudié *contabilidad*. Ya lo sé...¡*no tiene nada que ver con* mi profesión!

Laura: ¿Tiene la oportunidad de usar su español en su trabajo?

Ricky: Bueno, resulta que pronto voy a pasar un mes en México para *intercambiar* ideas sobre entrenamientos y métodos para controlar los incendios con el Servicio Forestal allá. ¡Estoy muy emocionado!

Laura: ¿A veces tiene usted miedo en su trabajo?

Ricky: Claro que sí, pero al mismo tiempo estoy tan concentrado que a veces me olvido del riesgo que existe. Me siento muy *afortunado* de ser parte de un *equipo* tan dedicado de hombres y mujeres. No sé qué haría sin ellos.

VOCABULARIO:

descarga de adrenalina - adrenaline rush   ***de turno*** - on duty   ***de guardia*** - on call
contabilidad - accounting   ***no tiene nada que ver con*** - it has nothing to do with
intercambiar - exchange   ***afortunado*** - lucky/fortunate   ***equipo*** - team

Enfoque de Carrera ◆ Discusión

A. Lee la entrevista en la página anterior en voz alta.

◆　◆　◆

B. Contesta las preguntas sobre la entrevista.

1. ¿A qué se dedica Ricky Mason? _____

2. ¿Dónde vive? _____

3. ¿Qué es lo que más le gusta de su trabajo? _____

4. ¿Qué es lo que menos le gusta? _____

5. ¿Qué estudió? _____

6. ¿Habla español en su trabajo?_____

7. ¿A veces tiene miedo en su trabajo?_____

8. ¿Qué piensa de su equipo? _____

◆　◆　◆

C. Ahora responde a las preguntas personales sobre este tema.

1. ¿Te gustaría ser bombero(a) paracaidista? Explica. _____

2. ¿Eres una persona que toma riesgos? _____

3. ¿Te da miedo el fuego? _____

4. ¿Te provoca alguna actividad una descarga de adrenalina? _____

5. ¿Por qué sería útil saber español en esta carrera? _____

◆　◆　◆

D. Comparte tus respuestas con la clase.

UNIDAD 3

El centro comercial

Shopping Center

1	**ROPA**
2	**DEPORTES/OCIO**
3	**SALUD/BELLEZA**
4	**HOGAR/COCINA**

❖ *Lección 1: La Ropa* (Clothes)

1 **Ropa** _____
mujeres, hombres, chicas, chicos, bebés

> **¿Cómo te queda esta chaqueta?**

> **Me queda bien. ¡Me la llevo!**

¡Ojo!

The verb *quedar* can be used to talk about how something fits.

Me queda bien la camisa.
The shirt fits well.

Me quedan grandes los zapatos.
The shoes are big on me.

Te queda grande la gorra.
The hat is big on you.

Te quedan apretados los pantalones.
The pants are tight on you.

talla	size	**estar de moda**	to be in fashion
de rebajas	on sale	**mostrar**	to show
apretado(a)	tight	**pagar**	to pay
cambiar	exchange	**ponerse**	to put on
comprar	to buy	**preferir**	to prefer
costar	to cost	**probar**	to try on
devolver	to return	**quedar bien/mal**	to fit well/poorly

🗣 PRACTICAR

1. a. Read the following dialogue out loud with a partner between a customer (***cliente(a)***) and a sales clerk (***dependiente(a)***):

Dependiente:	Hola señor. ¿Cómo puedo servirle?
Cliente:	Bueno, necesito zapatos nuevos para el trabajo.
Dependiente:	Puedo mostrarle unos zapatos que están de rebajas.
Cliente:	Sí, por favor. ¿Cuánto cuestan?
Dependiente:	Este fin de semana, están a $35. ¿Qué talla usa usted?
Cliente:	Uso un 42. Y los prefiero en negro, por favor.
Dependiente:	De acuerdo, un momento. [Pausa] Aquí los tiene.
Cliente:	Me quedan un poco apretados. ¿Puedo probar un 43?
Dependiente:	Sí, pero sólo tenemos el 43 en marrón. ¿Está bien?
Cliente:	Sí, está bien. Me los llevo. ¡Gracias!

b. Now, create your own dialogue using a different clothing theme.

Dependiente(a): _____

Cliente(a): _____

Dependiente(a): _____

Cliente(a): _____

Dependiente(a): _____

Cliente(a): _____

Dependiente(a): _____

Cliente(a): _____

Dependiente(a): _____

Cliente(a): _____

c. Exchange your completed dialogues with other classmates and perform each other's dialogues.

2. How often do you buy the following articles of clothing?

1 = Con mucha frecuencia
Frequently

3 = No mucho
Not a lot

2 = A veces
Sometimes

4 = Nunca
Never

1. ____ los zapatos

6. ____ un vestido

2. ____ una gorra

7. ____ una corbata

3. ____ una camiseta

8. ____ una chaqueta

4. ____ los calcetines

9. ____ una camisa

5. ____ un traje de baño

10. ____ unos vaqueros

3. Take turns asking each other about clothing preferences in different situations.

¿Prefieres...

1. ... llevar **pantalones largos** o **pantalones cortos** cuando hace fresco?

2. ... llevar **un traje/vestido elegante** o **ropa informal** cuando sales?

3. ... llevar **un abrigo largo** o **una chaqueta deportiva** cuando hace frío?

4. ... llevar **zapatos de ténis** o **botas** cuando caminas en el bosque?

5. ... levar una camisa de **manga larga** o de **manga corta**?

6. ... llevar **una gorra** o prefieres andar **sin gorra** cuando hace frío?

7. ...llevar **un paraguas** o **un impermeable y gorra**?

8. ...llevar sandalias **con calcetines** o **sin calcetines**?

¡Ojo!

Many of the verbs you have learned so far in the present tense are easily formed by cutting off the ending, and adding the following endings:

	hablar (to talk)	**comer** (to eat)	**vivir** (to live)
yo	habl**o**	com**o**	viv**o**
tú	habl**as**	com**es**	viv**es**
él, ella, usted	habl**a**	com**e**	viv**e**
nosotros(as)	habl**amos**	com**emos**	viv**imos**
vosotros(as)	habl**áis**	com**éis**	viv**ís**
ellos, ellas, Uds.	habl**an**	com**en**	viv**en**

Some verbs, called stem-changing verbs, have these same endings, but also have a change in the root. There are 3 types of stem-changing verbs:

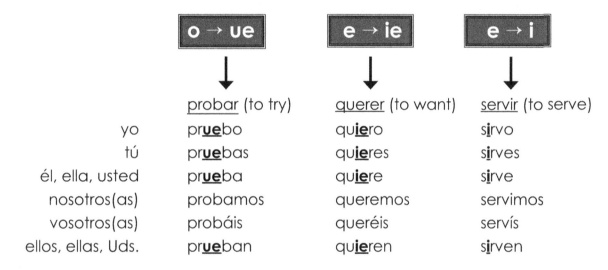

	o → ue	**e → ie**	**e → i**
	probar (to try)	querer (to want)	servir (to serve)
yo	pr**ue**bo	qu**ie**ro	s**i**rvo
tú	pr**ue**bas	qu**ie**res	s**i**rves
él, ella, usted	pr**ue**ba	qu**ie**re	s**i**rve
nosotros(as)	probamos	queremos	servimos
vosotros(as)	probáis	queréis	servís
ellos, ellas, Uds.	pr**ue**ban	qu**ie**ren	s**i**rven

Notice that the stem-change occurs everywhere but the ***nosotros*** and ***vosotros*** forms.

Other common **o → ue** stem-changing verbs:
    costar (to cost), **mostrar** (to show), **poder** (to be able/"can")

Other common **e → ie** stem-changing verbs:
    pensar (to think), **preferir** (to prefer), **cerrar** (to close)

Other common **e → i** stem-changing verbs:
    pedir (to order/ask for), **repetir** (to repeat), **decir** (to say/tell)

✏️ ESCRIBIR

A. Match the segments from the two columns to make logical statements and questions.

1. Esta camisa me queda...   ____   a. ...ponerme un abrigo.

2. Perdón. ¿Me puede mostrar... ____   b. ...porque no me quedan bien.

3. Estos zapatos están...   c. ...unos panatones negros?

4. Me gustan los pantalones...   ____   d. ...tarjeta de crédito.

5. Hace frío. Voy a...   ____   e. ...pero ¿cuánto cuestan?

6. Quiero devolver los zapatos... ____   f. ...grande. Voy a probar otra.

7. Prefiero pagar con...   ____   g. ...usas?

8. ¿Qué talla...   ____   h. ...de moda. ¡Y son cómodos!

B. Answer the following questions about your clothing shopping preferences and experiences in Spanish.

1. ¿Siempre pruebas la ropa antes de comprarla?

   _____

2. ¿Prefieres comprar ropa en una tienda pequeña, el centro comercial o en internet?

   _____

3. ¿Te gusta recibir ropa como un regalo?

   _____

4. ¿Qué ropa te pones cuando sales de noche?

   _____

5. ¿Tomas decisiones rápidas cuando vas de compras?

   _____

C. Form statements with each of the verbs in the column B with a corresponding subject in column A, and a logical item in column C.

<u>A</u>	<u>B</u>	<u>C</u>
Yo	**peferir** (e→ie)	gafas de sol
Nosotros	**probar** (o→ue)	una gorra
Ellas	**pensar** (e→ie)	unas botas
La tienda	**servir** (e→i)	una falda
Tú	**mostrar** (o→ue)	los pantalones
El dependiente	**querer** (e→ie)	otra talla
Tú y Eva	**comprar**	el verde
La cliente	**pedir** (e→i)	$75
Los clientes	**cerrar** (e→ie)	la tienda
La chaqueta	**devolver** (o→ue)	el traje de baño
Rodrigo	**costar** (o→ue)	al cliente

1. _____

2. _____

3. _____

4. _____

5. _____

6. _____

7. _____

8. _____

9. _____

10. _____

11. _____

❖ *Lección 2: Los deportes y el ocio*

(Sports and Leisure)

---

2 | **Deportes/Ocio**

equipo deportivo, juegos, juguetes, libros, electrónica

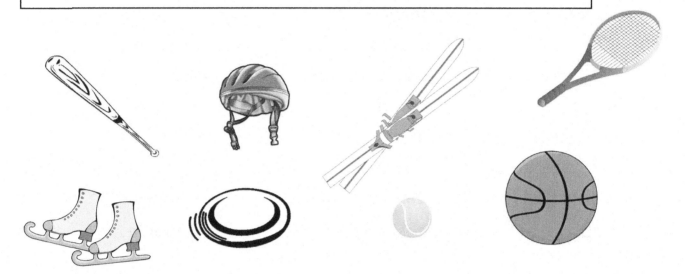

el balón	ball (big)	**el rompecabezas**	puzzle
el bate	bat	**las cartas/los naipes**	cards
la bici(cleta)	bike/bicycle	**el disco volador**	frisbee
el casco	helmet	**los juegos de mesa**	board games
los esquís	skis	**los libros de...**	books
el guante de béisbol	baseball glove	**...aventura**	...adventure
los patines	skates	**...suspenso**	...suspense
la pelota	ball (small)	**...romance**	...romance
la raqueta	racket	**...ciencia ficción**	...science fiction
la tabla de snowboard	snowboard	**la muñeca**	doll
		los videojuegos	video games

PRACTICAR ─────────────────────────

1. ¡LOTERÍA! Draw a picture of 16 of the items found in the Deportes/Ocio section on the previous page in the squares below. Then, play **¡LOTERÍA!**

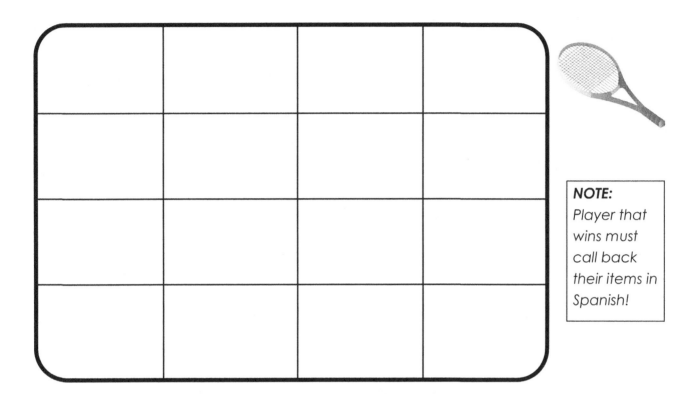

NOTE:
Player that wins must call back their items in Spanish!

2. a. First, assign the following prices to each of the following items. Your choice!

| $21 | $11 | $343 | $36 | $68 | $9 | $515 | $80 |

b. Compare your prices with those of a classmate, asking, **"¿Cuánto cuesta la raqueta?"**, and comment on each other's decisions, using the following phrases.

Está bien de precio.	*It's well priced.*
Es (demasiado) barato.	*It's (too) cheap.*
Es (demasiado) caro.	*It's (too) expensive.*

3. In pairs, take turns playing the roles of the customer and salesperson. After greeting each other, the customer will start by stating what he or she wants to do. The salesperson will then recommend something in the store. It will go something like this:

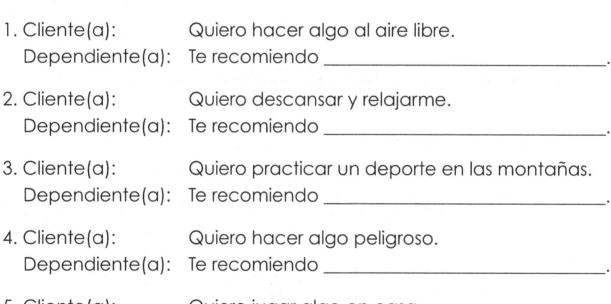

Cliente: **Quiero jugar al béisbol.**
Dependiente: **Te recomiendo __un bate y un guante.__**

1. Cliente(a):   Quiero hacer algo al aire libre.
   Dependiente(a):   Te recomiendo _____.

2. Cliente(a):   Quiero descansar y relajarme.
   Dependiente(a):   Te recomiendo _____.

3. Cliente(a):   Quiero practicar un deporte en las montañas.
   Dependiente(a):   Te recomiendo _____.

4. Cliente(a):   Quiero hacer algo peligroso.
   Dependiente(a):   Te recomiendo _____.

5. Cliente(a):   Quiero jugar algo en casa.
   Dependiente(a):   Te recomiendo _____.

6. Cliente(a):   Quiero hacer una actividad de concentración.
   Dependiente(a):   Te recomiendo _____.

✎ ESCRIBIR

A. Match the following Spanish sports and leisure terms in **Columna A** with the corresponding equipment in **Columna B**.

Columna A		Columna B
1. el fútbol	____	a. el bate
2. el ténis	____	b. el casco
3. el béisbol	____	c. el libro
4. leer	____	d. los patines
5. patinar	____	e. el balón
6. bicicleta	____	f. la raqueta

B. Read each of the following scenarios out loud and state what you need to buy or rent, with **Necesito comprar...** or **Necesito alquilar...** Look up any words in the dictionary that you do not know.

1. Quiero pasar un fin de semana en las montañas, haciendo algo divertido, pero también quiero relajarme y descansar.

   _____

2. Hoy no quiero salir de la casa ni por un minuto.

   _____

3. Esta semana quiero practicar un deporte muy activo y quizás un poco peligroso.

   _____

4. Mañana quiero practicar un deporte de estrategia.

   _____

5. No soy bueno(a) con las manos pero tengo las piernas fuertes.

   _____

C. Based on ***Activity B*** on the previous page, state that you like to do each of the associated activities with **Me gusta...**, and then what you're going to need in order to do the activity with **Voy a necesitar...**

    Por ejemplo: Me gusta leer y voy a necesitar un libro.

1. _____

2. _____

3. _____

4. _____

5. _____

In the previous activity, you used **Me gusta...** to state *I like to...* You've also learned **¿Te gusta...?** to ask *Do you like to...*

In order to talk about what someone else likes to do, you will use **Le gusta...**

    Por ejemplo: <u>Le gusta</u> jugar al fútbol. *He/She likes to play soccer.*

To be more specific about who it is that likes to do something, you simply state the person in a phrase with "a".

    Por ejemplo:

        <u>**A Raúl**</u> le gusta ir de compras.   *Raul likes to shop.*

        <u>**A mi hermana**</u> le gusta esquiar. *My sister likes to ski.*

D. Form sentences about what the following people like to do.

    Por ejemplo: mi vecino / patinar → A mi vecino le gusta patinar.

1. María / ir al gimnasio_____

2. mi madre / escalar _____

3. mi amigo / jugar al béisbol _____

4. Juan / leer_____

5. el cliente / comprar ropa _____

❖ *Lección 3: La salud y la belleza*

(Health and Beauty)

---

3 **Salud y Belleza**

peluquería, gimnasio, spa, maquillaje

Para mi día de salud y belleza, prefiero ir...

For my health and beauty day, I prefer to go...

al spa

a la peluquería

al gimnasio

la barbería	barber shop	la pedicura	pedicure
la gimnasio	gym	la peluquería	hair salon
la manicura	manicure	las pesas	weights
el maquillaje	makeup	la sauna	sauna
el masaje	massage	el yoga	yoga

 PRACTICAR

1. **¿En qué consiste tu día ideal de salud y belleza?** What does your ideal day of health and beauty consist of?

   a. Ask three people this question, and write their name in the corresponding column.

la peluquería	el gimnasio	el spa	otro

   b. Then, ask each person what they like to do at each place.

   ¿Qué te gusta hacer en el/la...?
   - Me gusta...

   c. Now, tell your group where each person likes to go. You can add what each person likes to do in those locations, as well.

   A Rachel le gusta levantar pesas en el gimnasio.

Las Preposiciones

Susana   *Maricel*   *Sofía*

Maricel está **entre** Susana y Sofía.	*Maricel is between Susana and Sofia.*
Las revistas están **encima de** los regazos.	*The magazines are on top of the laps.*
Los pies están **en** el agua.	*Their feet are in the water.*
Las sillas están **sobre** las tinas de agua.	*The chairs are over the tubs of water.*
Las tinas están **debajo de** las sillas.	*The tubs are under the chairs.*
Sofía está **a la derecha de** Maricel.	*Sofia is to the right of Maricel.*
Susana está **a la izquierda de** Maricel.	*Susana is to the left of Maricel.*

a la derecha de	to the right of	**en**	in, on
a la izquierda de	to the left of	**encima de**	on top of
al lado de	next to	**enfrente de**	in front of
debajo de	under	**entre**	between
detrás de	behind	**sobre**	over

2. In groups of 3, arrange yourselves in chairs, like in the drawing above, pretending to have your feet in water. Repeat the sentences above, using your names.

3. In small groups, take turns making statements about where various items are in the room, using the prepositions above. The others in your group will guess what the item is based on the clues given.

✏️ ESCRIBIR

A. Answer the following questions about your habits and preferences concerning *la salud y la belleza*.

1. ¿Cuántas veces vas a la peluqería al año?

_____

2. ¿Hablas mucho con el/la peluquero(a)?

_____

3. ¿Prefieres hacer ejercicio afuera o en el gimnasio?

_____

4. ¿Cuál es tu ejercicio favorito que haces?

_____

5. ¿Fuiste una vez a un spa? ¿Qué hiciste allí?

_____

6. ¿Te interesa más una pedicura, una manicura, un masaje o ninguno de los tres? _____

B. Answer the following questions about the location of various things in the room, using as many prepositions as you can.

1. ¿Dónde está el reloj?   _____

2. ¿Dónde está el/la maestro(a)? _____

3. ¿Dónde están tus libros? _____

4. ¿Dónde está el escritorio? _____

5. ¿Dónde está tu compañero(a) de clase? _____

C. Complete the following sentences about the location of the people and things in the drawing above, using the correct prepositions.

al lado	enfrente	encima	debajo	sobre

a la derecha	a la izquierda	entre	en	detrás

1. Mary está _____ de Bill.

2. Las nubes están _____ los edificios.

3. Los edificios están _____ de las nubes.

4. Mary, Bill y Sandy están _____ de la bicicleta fija.

5. Sandy está _____ de la planta.

6. Sandy está _____ de Bill.

7. Mary, Bill y Sandy están _____ el gimnasio.

8. Bill está _____ Mary y Sandy.

9. La planta está _____ de Sandy.

10. Bill está _____ de Mary.

❖ Lección 4: El hogar y la cocina
(Home and Kitchen)

4 **Hogar y Cocina**

aparatos domésticos, baño, cocina, habitación

¿Qué piensas comprar? *What do you plan on buying?*

— Pienso comprar... *I plan on buying...*

...una aspiradora.

...una batidora.

...un sartén.

...jabón.

La Cocina (Kitchen)

la cafetera	coffee maker
la estufa/la cocina	stove
el horno	oven
el lavaplatos	dishwasher
la licuadora/batidora	blender, mixer
el microondas	microwave
el refrigerador/la nevera	refrigerator
el sartén	skillet
la tostadora	toaster

El Dormitorio (Bedroom)

la almohada	pillow
el despertador	alarm clock
las sábanas	sheets

El Cuarto de Baño (Bathroom)

el cepillo de dientes	toothbrush
el champú	shampoo
el espejo	mirror
el jabón	soap
el papel higiénico	toilet paper
la toalla	towel

Misc. (Misc.)

la aspiradora	vacuum cleaner
la escoba	broom
la lámpara	lamp
la lavadora	washing machine
la secadora	dryer
el televisor	television set

PRACTICAR ————————————————————

1. a. In small groups, practice the vocabulary on the previous page, taking turns asking, "¿Dónde está...el jabón?, and responding "El jabón está en el cuarto de baño.", etc.

b. Once you become more familiar with the vocabulary, perform the same activity as above, but quizzing each other this time, with the person responding not looking at the book.

c. Now, take turns asking each other where the following items are, and responding with the appropriate appliance or kitchen ware.

Por ejemplo: ¿Dónde están los huevos?   — Están en el sartén.

1. la toalla

2. la leche

3. las palomitas

4. el café

5. las galletas

6. el pan

7. los platos

8. el panqueque

You've already used the verb ***tener*** (to have) in several of the lessons. Let's review the verb in all its forms:

¡Ojo!

	<u>tener</u> (to have)
yo	**tengo**
tú	**tienes**
él, ella, usted	**tiene**
nosotros(as)	**tenemos**
vosotros(as)	**tenéis**
ellos, ellas, ustedes	**tienen**

2. ¿Qué necesitamos? You just moved to Ecuador and your family needs some things for the new apartment. With a partner, take turns asking if something is needed, and responding with the indicated response, according to the following model:

¿Necesitamos sábanas? (Do we need sheets?)
— No, ya tenemos sábanas. (No, we already have sheets.)

1.

2.

3.

4.

5.

6.

7.

8.

9.

10.

ESCRIBIR

A. Complete the crossword puzzle based on the clues below.

CRUCIGRAMA (Hogar y Cocina)

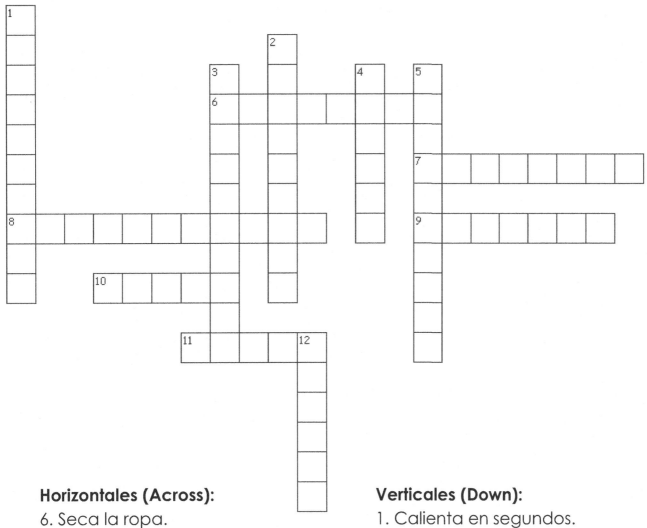

Horizontales (Across):
6. Seca la ropa.
7. Para la cabeza.
8. ¡Despiértate!
9. Da luz.
10. Está caliente.
11. Te hace limpio

Verticales (Down):
1. Calienta en segundos.
2. Hace batidos.
3. Limpia y hace mucho ruido.
4. Seca los platos y el cuerpo.
5. Lava los platos.
12. Está frío.

B. Asociaciones Circle the item that does not belong in the following groups. Share and explain your answers with a classmate, in Spanish.

1. a. lavaplatos   b. lavadora   c. aspiradora   d. horno
2. a. espejo   b. sartén   c. horno   d. estufa
3. a. sábanas   b. tostadora   c. almohada   d. lámpara
4. a. cafetera   b. licuadora   c. escoba   d. tostadora
5. a. tostadora   b. almohada   c. sábanas   d. despertador

C. ¿Con qué frecuencia? State how frequently you use the following items, using ***todos los días, frecuentemente, a veces, pocas veces, nunca***.

Por ejemplo: **la estufa** → Uso la estufa todos los días.

1. **el sartén** _____
2. **el microondas** _____
3. **el espejo** _____
4. **la lavadora** _____
5. **la cafetera** _____
6. **el despertador** _____
7. **el televisor** _____
8. **la aspiradora** _____
9. **la tostadora** _____
10. **el horno** _____

D. Ask your classmates about their habits above, using the question, **¿Con qué frecuencia usas...?** Compare the answers with yours.

❖ *Lección 5: El Repaso* (Review)

A. Match the Spanish words with the English counterparts.

1. cuesta	____	a.	puzzle	
2. casco	____	b.	we pay	
3. almohada	____	c.	ball	
4. rompecabezas	____	d.	makeup	
5. patines	____	e.	vacuum cleaner	
6. peluquería	____	f.	doll	
7. escoba	____	g.	they try (on)	
8. despertador	____	h.	pillow	
9. pelota	____	i.	helmet	
10. gimnasio	____	j.	dishwasher	
11. maquillaje	____	k.	alarm clock	
12. sartén	____	l.	hair salon/barber shop	
13. pagamos	____	m.	skates	
14. devuelvo	____	n.	gym	
15. entre	____	o.	mirror	
16. espejo	____	p.	it costs	
17. aspiradora	____	q.	I return (an object)	
18. prueban	____	r.	skillet	
19. muñeca	____	s.	broom	
20. lavaplatos	____	t.	between	

B. Ask 2 or 3 classmates about the last time they went to the mall. Include:

1. ¿Cuándo fue la última vez que fuiste al centro comercial?
2. ¿Compraste algo o fuiste sólo para mirar?
3. ¿Prefieres comprar ropa en el centro comercial o una tienda?
4. ¿Cuánto tiempo te gusta pasar en un centro comercial?

Enfoque de Carrera

Músico
31 años
Louisville, KY

Kate Hargadon

Laura: Hola Kate. No le voy a robar mucho tiempo porque sé que usted necesita preparar para el concierto esta noche. ¿Me puede decir desde cuando toca como profesional?

Kate: Bueno, *llevo toda la vida tocando* varios instrumentos y cantando pero llevo unos 8 años como profesional.

Laura: ¿Qué es lo que más le gusta de su trabajo?

Kate: Me gusta la conexión con la gente durante ciertos momentos provocada por mi música. Me inspira mucho.

Laura: ¿Qué es lo que menos le gusta de su trabajo?

Kate: Es una pregunta difícil porque me gusta mucho mi profesión, pero ya no me gusta viajar tanto. Los días de tanto *movimiento* ya se están reduciendo.

Laura: ¿Tiene usted la oportunidad de usar su español durante el trabajo?

Kate: He tenido unas experiencias muy lindas, colaborando con músicos latinos. Me gusta mucho experimentar con varias *fusiones* de *ritmos*, incluyendo ritmos latinos. Y para conocerlos bien, tengo que viajar a Latinamérica. Ya lo sé, ¡es un trabajo *duro*!

Laura: ¿Qué tipo de música prefiere tocar?

Kate: Mi pasión es el jazz pero nunca me niego a tocar cualquier tipo de música.

Laura: Bueno, tengo ganas de escuchar su música esta noche. Gracias por su tiempo, Kate.

Kate: Fue un placer, Laura. Gracias por su interés.

VOCABULARIO:

No le voy a robar mucho tiempo - I'm not going to take a lot of your time
llevo toda la vida tocando - I've been playing my whole life   ***movimiento*** - movement
fusiones - fusions   ***ritmos*** - rhythms   ***duro*** - hard   ***nunca me niego*** - I never refuse

Enfoque de Carrera ◆ Discusión

A. Lee la entrevista en la página anterior en voz alta.

B. Contesta las preguntas sobre la entrevista.

1. ¿A qué se dedica Kate Hargadon? _____

2. ¿Cuánto tiempo lleva siendo músico? _____

3. ¿Dónde vive? _____

4. ¿Qué es lo que más le gusta de su trabajo? _____

5. ¿Qué es lo que menos le gusta? _____

6. ¿Habla español en su trabajo? _____

7. ¿Qué tipo de música toca? _____

◆ ◆ ◆

C. Ahora responde a las preguntas personales sobre este tema.

1. ¿Tocas algún instrumento?_____

2. ¿Qué tipo de música te gusta? _____

3. ¿Qué instrumento te gustaría aprender a tocar?_____

4. ¿Te gustaría ser músico algún día? _____

5. ¿Por qué sería útil saber español en esta carrera? _____

◆ ◆ ◆

D. Comparte tus respuestas con la clase.

UNIDAD

El medio ambiente

The Environment

❖ *Lección 1: El ciclo del agua*
(Water Cycle)

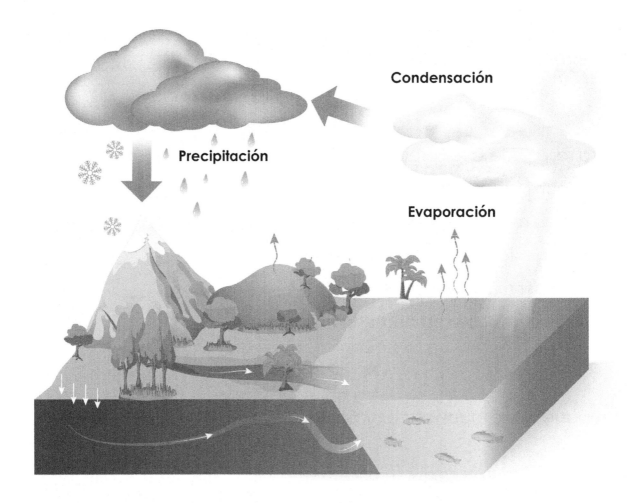

Condensación

Precipitación

Evaporación

¿Cuáles son las partes del ciclo del agua?

① **La evaporación**
consiste en...

② **La condensación**
consiste en...

③ **La precipitación**
consiste en...

el vapor / el sol / el agua	las nubes / el sol / el agua	las nubes / la nieve / la lluvia

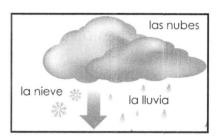

 PRACTICAR ──────────────────────

1. First, your teacher will say the terms above several times, first slowly to carefully distinguish between the syllables, and then increasing to a natural speed. Repeat, paying special attention to the vowels:

   evaporación → eh - vah - poh - rah - syon
   condensación → cohn - dehn - sah - syon
   precipitación → preh - see - pee - tah - syon

2. Your teacher will describe the phases of the water cycle, using words and gestures. Circle the phase as it is described. Some useful words you might hear are:

   sube - *rises*   **baja** - *falls/goes down*   **calienta** - *heats*   **mar** - *sea*
   nieva - *it snows*   **llueve** - *rains*   **ríos** - *rivers*   **lagos** - *lakes*
   nube - *cloud*   **agua** - *water*   **formación** - *formation*

   1. a. evaporación   b. condensación   c. precipitación

   2. a. evaporación   b. condensación   c. precipitación

   3. a. evaporación   b. condensación   c. precipitación

✎ ESCRIBIR

A. **Ciclo del agua.** Draw your own water cycle, including labels in Spanish for the following natural features and processes (use arrows to show in which direction they move):

la nube   el sol   la nieve   la lluvia   el río   el lago   el mar
la evaporación   la condensación   la precipitación

B. **Seleccionar.** Select the word that best completes the following statements.

1. Un ejemplo de precipitación es...

    a. la nube   b. la evaporación   c. la lluvia   d. el lago

2. La evaporación consiste en...

    a. el vapor   b. la condensación   c. la nieve   d. la lluvia

3. El sol es necesario para...

    a. la lluvia   b. la precipitación   c. la evaporación d. la nieve

The verbs **SUBIR** and **BAJAR** are very common and highly variable in their usage: SUBIR - "to go up", "to rise", "to raise", "to get on" (bus)
                    BAJAR - "to go down", "to lower", "to get down", "to get off" (bus)

¡Ojo!

	<u>subir</u>	<u>bajar</u>
yo	subo	bajo
tú	subes	bajas
él, ella, usted	sube	baja
nosotros(as)	subimos	bajamos
vosotros(as)	subís	bajáis
ellos, ellas, ustedes	suben	bajan

Examples of **SUBIR** and **BAJAR** in different contexts:

El vapor **sube** rápido cuando hace mucho sol.
*The vapor **rises** fast when it's very sunny.*

Subimos la montaña para llegar al lago.
*We **go up** the mountain to get to the lake.*

Ellos **bajan** la escalera con cuidado porque hay un escalón roto.
They go down the stairs carefully because there's a broken step.

Mi madre siempre **baja** las persianas cuando hace mucho sol.
*My mother always **lowers** the blinds when it's really sunny.*

C. Completar. Fill in the blank with the correct verb form of **SUBIR** or **BAJAR**, as necessary.

1. El río _____ la montaña hasta llegar al mar.

2. Nosotros _____ la cuesta lentamente, y luego,

   _____ la cuesta rápidamente.

3. El vapor _____ hacia el cielo y forma nubes.

4. Los niños _____ el árbol para esconderse *(to hide)*.

5. Yo _____ del autobús en la calle 11 y camino a casa.

❖ *Lección 2: La contaminación*
(Pollution)

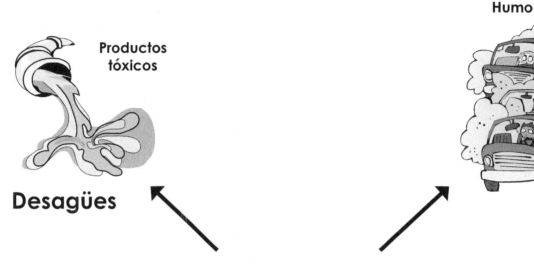

Productos tóxicos

Desagües

Humo

Coches

Tipos de contaminación

Humo

Fábricas

Basura

Vertidos ilegales

la basura	litter/garbage	**el humo**	smoke/exhaust
los coches/carros	cars	**el medio ambiente**	environment
la contaminación	pollution	**los productos tóxicos**	toxic products
la fábrica	factory	**el vertido ilegal**	illegal dumping
el desagüe	drain		

PRACTICAR

1. With a partner, talk about your general impressions of pollution in Spanish. The vocabulary on the previous page may be useful, along with these words:

feo   peligroso   costoso   malo para la salud   lluvia ácida

Can you figure out what the words mean? How does the last term relate to the *ciclo del agua* from the previous lesson?

2. How does pollution effect the following people, animals and places? Your class will be divided into various groups, and will discuss pollution issues for each group. Take notes in your column, and then fill out other columns when your classmates share their ideas.

pájaro	obrero(a)	bosque	pez	río

3. In small groups, talk about some possible solutions for the pollution problems mentioned above. Take notes, as ideas are discussed.

_____

_____

_____

_____

✎ ESCRIBIR

A. Antes y después. Draw before and after scenes of pollution and clean-up scenes on water (*agua*), on land (*tierra*), and in the air (*aire*). Label in Spanish.

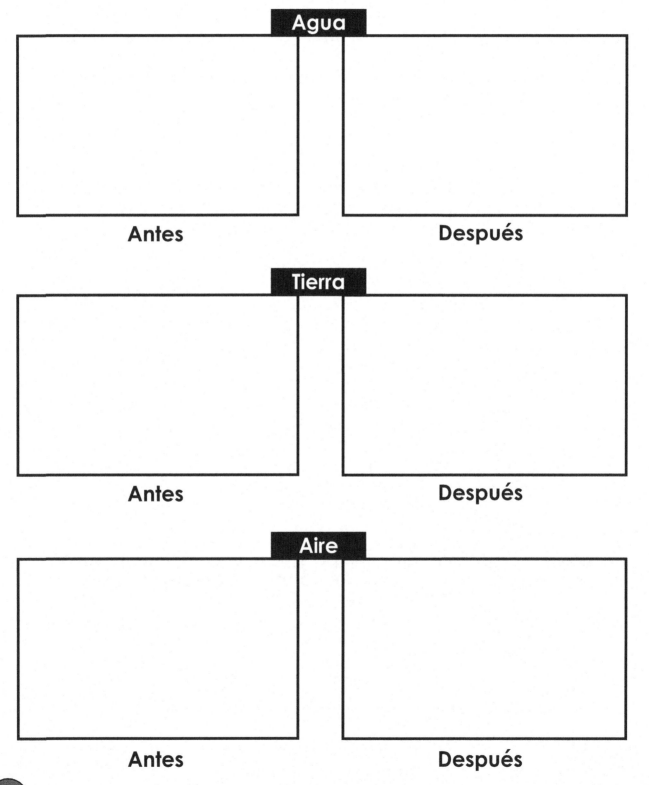

Agua

Antes   Después

Tierra

Antes   Después

Aire

Antes   Después

Commands are a part of everyday conversation, as we often need to tell someone to do something. For example, "Call me later.", "Close the door when you leave.", "Go to bed early.", etc.

• To form an informal command in Spanish, use the same verb form as in the él, ella, usted present tense. Por ejemplo:

andar	→	<u>Anda</u> en bicicleta.	*Ride your bike.*
usar	→	<u>Usa</u> productos naturales.	*Use natural products.*
comer	→	<u>Come</u> comida orgánica.	*Eat organic food.*

* There are some irregular affirmative commands. Here are a few:

hacer → **haz**	poner → **pon**	salir → **sal**	decir → **di**
<u>Haz</u> la tarea.	<u>Pon</u> el té aquí.	¡<u>Sal</u> ya!	<u>Di</u> la verdad.
Do the homework.	*Put the tea here.*	*Leave now!*	*Tell the truth.*

• To form a negative informal command, you first need to change the last vowel of the verb in the "yo" form to the "opposite vowel" ("**e**" for -ar ending verbs and "**a**" for -er and -ir ending verbs), and then add an "s". Por ejemplo:

usar	→	<u>No uses</u> mucho el coche.	*Don't use the car a lot.*
arrojar	→	<u>No arrojes</u> basura al suelo.	*Don't litter.*
comer	→	<u>No comas</u> mucho azúcar.	*Don't eat a lot of sugar.*

B. Mandatos. Practice forming commands with the following verbs, according to the model.

Affirmative commands: hablar → Habla.

1. reciclar _____   3. comer _____

2. comprar _____   4. beber _____

Negative commands: hablar → No hables.

1. arrojar _____   3. comer _____

2. manejar _____   4. beber _____

C. Publicidad. Make posters about pollution and helping the environment. Use commands, both in the affirmative and negative (see previous page). First, write out some possible ones here that you may use on your poster below.

<u>Affirmative Commands</u>

_____

_____

_____

_____

_____

<u>Negative Commands</u>

_____

_____

_____

_____

_____

❖ *Lección 3: El reciclaje (Recycling)*

¿Qué reciclamos?

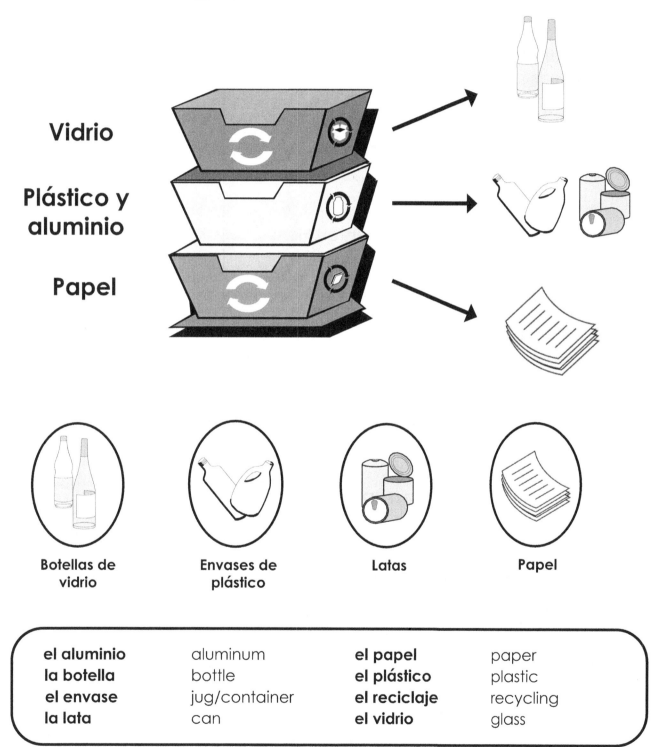

Botellas de vidrio	**Envases de plástico**	**Latas**	**Papel**

el aluminio	aluminum	**el papel**	paper
la botella	bottle	**el plástico**	plastic
el envase	jug/container	**el reciclaje**	recycling
la lata	can	**el vidrio**	glass

🗣 PRACTICAR ──────────────

1. Your teacher will hold up various items. For each one, state in which recycling container **(contenedor)** it belongs. For example:

Una botella de plástico   →   **va al contenedor de plástico.**

If it's not recyclable, then state that it goes to the "vertedero" (landfill).

Un pañal (diaper)   →   **va al vertedero.**

 ¡Ojo! Many communities collect food waste, which is then turned into compost, an organic material. In Spanish it is referred to as "**orgánico**".

2. Your classroom is a recycling center! Here's how it works:

a. Each student creates one card for each of the following items below. Draw a picture or paste a cut-out of an example of each category.

1. **Plástico**   2. **Vidrio**   3. **Aluminio**

4. **Papel**   5. **Orgánico**   6. **Vertedero**

b. Your teacher will designate teams of garbage collectors for each of these categories. As they pass by, they'll ask you if you have anything for their container:

¿Tienes algo para...   plástico, papel, vidrio, etc.?
Do you have something for...   plastic, paper, glass, etc.?

c. Once all the waste is collected, each of the garbage collector teams will announce what they have collected. The class will confirm that the waste was collected in the appropriate containers.

✏️ ESCRIBIR ───────────────────────

A. **¿Reciclable o no?** Place the list of items in the appropriate recycling column, or vertedero (landfill). Look up any words you do not know.

pilas	envase de yogur	bote de mayonesa	colchón
periódico	lata de refresco	botella de vino	revista
cartón de huevos	pañal	envoltorio de caramelo	correo
servilleta	guía telefónica	caja de cereal	envase de helado
aceite de coche	lata de pintura	cáscara de huevos	bombilla
papel de aluminio	planta muerta	bolsa de papel	poliestireno

PAPEL	PLÁSTICO	ALUMINIO	VIDRIO	ORGÁNICO
1.	1.	1.	1.	1.
2.	2.	2.	2.	2.
3.	3.	3.	3.	3.
4.	4.	4.	4.	4.
5.	5.	5.	5.	5.
6.	6.	6.	6.	6.
7.	7.	7.	7.	7.
8.	8.	8.	8.	8.

VERTEDERO

1. _____
2. _____
3. _____
4. _____
5. _____
6. _____
7. _____
8. _____

B. ¡Menos basura! Observe what is in the *vertedero*, as well as other containers and list alternatives to these items, as to reduce the amount of waste. Use the model below to create sentences.

Por ejemplo: **botella de plástico**

→ **En vez de usar** botellas de plástico, podemos usar nuestras propias botellas.

Instead of using plastic bottles, we can use our own bottles.

1. _____ _____
   artículo *(item)*   alternativa

2. _____ _____
   artículo *(item)*   alternativa

3. _____ _____
   artículo *(item)*   alternativa

4. _____ _____
   artículo *(item)*   alternativa

5. _____ _____
   artículo *(item)*   alternativa

In the previous exercise, you may have noticed that to express, "instead of + ing", you leave the verb in the infinitive, in Spanish.

Por ejemplo: **En vez de usar** botellas de plástico...
Instead of using plastic bottles...

This same rule applies to any phrase with "de" with a verb that follows:

Depués de comer, voy a la tienda.
After eating, I'm going to the store.

Antes de salir, tienes que sacar la basura.
Before leaving, you have to take out the garbage.

Somos capaces de reciclar.
We are capable of recycling.

C. Completar. Fill in the blank with the appropriate verb in the word bank. What do these statements mean?

reciclar	comprar	usar	lavar	tirar	decidir

1. Antes de _____ algo en la tienda, es bueno saber si es reciclable.

2. En vez de _____ una lata a la basura, puedes reciclarla.

3. ¿Eres capaz de _____ los materiales de plástico y vidrio en tu vecindario *(neighborhood)*?

4. No es necesario _____ los platos de papel antes de ponerlos en el contenedor de "orgánico".

5. Después de _____ los envases, los pones en el contenedor.

6. Es bueno _____ comprar cosas reciclabes.

D. ¿Lo necesitas? For some things that we find in our garbage, we can find alternatives. For other things, we don't think we could live without. State your position for each of the following items.

Por ejemplo: un envase de poliestireno *(a Styrofoam container)*
¡Lo* necesito!   o   No lo* necesito. Puedo usar un plato.

*Use the appropriate direct object pronoun according to each item: **lo, la, los, las**

1. bolsas de plástico   _____

2. envoltorios de dulces   _____

3. papel de aluminio   _____

4. bombillas   _____

5. pilas   _____

6. pañales desechables   _____

❖ *Lección 4: Vivir verde* (Living Green)

Cómo cuidar el planeta

plantar un árbol

usar bolsas reutilizables

apagar la luz cuando no la usas

andar en bicicleta como transporte

no echar productos tóxicos

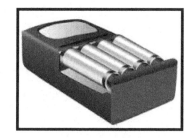

usar pilas recargables

apagar	to turn off	**la bolsa reutilizable**	reusable bag
echar	to throw out	**la luz/las luces**	light(s)
plantar	to plant	**las pilas**	batteries
reducir	to reduce	**los productos tóxicos**	toxic products
(re)usar	to (re)use	**el transporte**	transportation

PRACTICAR

1. In small groups, ask your classmates questions about their environmental practices.

1. ¿Qué tipo de bolsas usas cuando vas de compras?
2. ¿Apagaste las luces en tu habitación esta mañana?
3. ¿Qué tipo de pilas usas?
4. ¿Plantaste un árbol o un arbusto *(bush)* alguna vez *(ever)*?
5. ¿A veces caminas o andas en bicicleta como transporte?

¡Ojo!

In number 4 above, you are asking a question in the preterite tense, "¿Plantaste alguna vez un árbol?", meaning "Did you ever plant a tree?"

You could also ask the question with the **present perfect**, "Have you ever planted a tree?", consisting of two parts, the present tense of the verb **haber** and the **past participle**, which is typically expressed with -ed in English:

Yo	he
Tú	has
Él, Ella, Ud.	ha
Nosotros(as)	hemos
Vosotros(as)	habéis
Ellos, Ellas, Uds.	han

+

plant**ado** un árbol. (-ar verbs → -ado)

reduc**ido** la basura. (-er, -ir verbs → -ido)*

Some irregular past participles*:			
abrir	→ **abierto**	hacer	→ **hecho**
decir	→ **dicho**	poner	→ **puesto**
escribir	→ **escrito**	ver	→ **visto**

Ejemplos:

¿**Has plantado** un árbol alguna vez?   *Have you ever planted a tree?*

Marta **ha visto** la contaminación.   *Marta has seen pollution.*

Ellos **han usado** pilas recargables.   *They have used rechargeable batteries.*

¿**Habéis reducido la basura**?   *Have you all reduced the trash?*

He apagado las luces esta semana.   *I have turned off the lights this week.*

¿Dónde **hemos puesto** la basura?   *Where have we put the garbage?*

2. In pairs, take turns asking if the other has ever done the following things.

1. ¿Has plantado un árbol alguna vez?

2. ¿Has subido un árbol alguna vez?

3. ¿Has andado en bicicleta como transporte alguna vez?

4. ¿Has comido grillos *(crickets)* alguna vez?

5. ¿Has usado una bolsa reutilizable alguna vez?

6. ¿Has usado pilas recargables alguna vez?

7. ¿Has hecho la tarea en papel reciclado alguna vez?

8. ¿Has visto una película 3-D alguna vez?

✏ ESCRIBIR

A. Answer the questions below about what you did yesterday (**ayer**), what you're doing today (**hoy**), and what you're doing tomorrow (**mañana**).

¿Qué hiciste ayer?

 - Planté un árbol ayer.

 - _____

 - _____

 - _____

¿Qué haces hoy?

 - Uso una bolsa reutilzable hoy.

 - _____

 - _____

 - _____

¿Qué vas a hacer mañana?

 -Voy a apagar las luces mañana.

 - _____

 - _____

 - _____

B. Fill in the blanks below, according to the prompts, **without looking at the story**. Then, copy your answers in the corresponding blanks in the story. Read your story out loud in groups or in front of the class.

1. _____ tu nombre - your name
2. _____ un lugar - a place with definite article
3. _____ algo vivo - something alive
4. _____ un color - a color
5. _____ una cosa - a plural thing no article
6. _____ algo que se mueve - something that moves with def. article
7. _____ una cosa *singular* - a singular thing with definite article
8. _____ un adjetivo *masculino singular*- masculine/singular adjective
9. _____ miembro de la familia - family member with no article
10. _____ material - material with no article
11. _____ verbo en el infinitivo - verb in the infinitive
12. _____ verbo en el infinitivo - verb in the infinitive
13. _____ mandato informal - informal command

¡Hola! Me llamo ¹_____ y soy estudiante en ²_____. Quiero hacer algo bueno para el medio ambiente. Pienso plantar un ³_____ porque hay poco ⁴_____ en mi barrio. Mi familia y yo ya usamos ⁵_____ reutilizables cuando vamos de compras. Pero usamos ⁶_____ demasiado *(too much)* y no andamos en bici ni tomamos el autobús lo suficiente.

Intentamos reciclar todo lo posible, como el papel, el plástico, ⁷_____ y el material ⁸_____. Mi ⁹_____ lleva pañales *(diapers)* de ¹⁰_____, así que éstos van al vertedero. Todos somos capaces de ¹¹_____ la basura que producimos. Antes de ¹²_____ algo, deberíamos *(we should)* considerar bien si lo necesitamos o no. Mi lema *(motto)* para este año es: ¡Reduce, recicla y ¹³_____!

Optional activity: Re-write the story with more logical answers on a separate sheet.

❖ *Lección 5: El Repaso* *(Review)*

A. Match the Spanish words with the English counterparts.

1. la luz	____	a.	glass
2. el coche	____	b.	bottle
3. el vidrio	____	c.	battery
4. la lata	____	d.	bag
5. la contaminación	____	e.	smoke/exhaust
6. la fábrica	____	f.	aluminum
7. la pila	____	g.	dump, landfill
8. la basura	____	h.	drain
9. el envase	____	i.	pollution
10. la botella	____	j.	factory
11. el medio ambiente	____	k.	environment
12. el humo	____	l.	condensation
13. el plástico	____	m.	light
14. el desagüe	____	n.	container
15. la bolsa	____	o.	recycling
16. la condensación	____	p.	evaporation
17. el vertedero	____	q.	plastic
18. el reciclaje	____	r.	can
19. el aluminio	____	s.	garbage, trash
20. la evaporación	____	t.	car

B. a. Ask 2 or 3 classmates the following questions about their routine:

    1. ¿Cuándo fue la última vez que caminaste a la tienda?

    2. ¿Qué reciclas?

    3. ¿Prefieres botellas o latas?

    b. Tell a classmate to do something, using a command form of the verb.

Enfoque de Carrera

Geóloga
52 años
Bellingham, WA

Liz Debari

Laura: Hola Liz. Gracias por la oportunidad de hablar con usted. Primero, la carrera de geología es grande. ¿Cuál es su especialidad?

Liz: Sí, Laura. Me especializo en vulcanología, o sea, el estudio de volcanes.

Laura: Interesante. ¿Qué es lo que más le gusta de su trabajo?

Liz: Lo que más me gusta es que paso la *mayor parte del tiempo* al aire libre, y muchas veces los lugares son muy bonitos. He estado en montañas en varias partes del mundo e incluso aquí muy cerca de mi casa, hay un volcán que se llama Mount Baker.

Laura: ¿Qué es lo que menos le gusta de su trabajo?

Liz: No me gusta *solicitar becas*, y tengo que pasar varias semanas al año haciendo eso.

Laura: ¿Tiene usted la oportunidad de usar su español en el trabajo?

Liz: Sí, uso mi español mucho, especialmente cuando hago investigaciones en Ecuador y Chile. A veces hay intérpretes pero cuando puedo prefiero hablar directamente con los miembros de mi equipo.

Laura: ¿Cuál es su palabra favorita en español?

Liz: Mi palabra favorita es *almohada* aunque no tiene nada que ver con la geología.

Laura: ¡Jajaja! Gracias por su tiempo, Liz. Le deseo mucho éxito en su trabajo.

Liz: Fue un placer, Laura. Chao.

VOCABULARIO:

terreno - field (study)   *o sea* - in other words   *mayor parte del tiempo* - most of the time
al aire libre - outdoors   *solicitar becas* - write grants   *almohada* - pillow

Enfoque de Carrera ◆ Discusión

A. Lee la entrevista en la página anterior en voz alta.

B. Contesta las preguntas sobre la entrevista.

1. ¿A qué se dedica Liz Debari? _____

2. ¿Cuántos años tiene? _____

3. ¿Qué es lo que más le gusta de su trabajo? _____

4. ¿Hay un volcán cerca de donde vive? _____

5. ¿Qué es lo que menos le gusta? _____

6. ¿Habla español en su trabajo? _____

7. ¿Necesita un intérprete? _____

8. ¿Cuál es su palabra favorita en español? _____

C. Ahora responde a las preguntas personales sobre este tema.

1. ¿Te gusta pasar tiempo en las montañas? _____

2. ¿Has visto un volcán alguna vez? _____

3. ¿Te gustaría trabajar al aire libre o en un oficina? _____

4. ¿Te interesa la carrera de geología? _____

5. ¿Por qué sería útil saber español en esta carrera? _____

D. Comparte tus respuestas con la clase.

UNIDAD

5

La tecnología

Technology

❖ *Lección 1: La televisión* (Television)

¿Qué hay en la tele?

What's on TV?

Deportes

Programas de la vida real

Dibujos animados

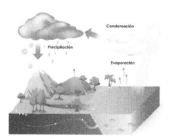

Programas educativos

las comedias	comedies (sitcoms)
los concursos	game shows
los deportes	sports
los dibujos animados	cartoons
los noticieros	news shows
los programas de la vida real	reality shows
los programas educativos	educational programs
las telenovelas	soap operas
las (tele)series	TV series

 PRACTICAR ─────────────────────

1. In pairs, guess what kind of programs you think the following titles are:

¿Qué tipo de programa es...?   **Creo que es un(a)...**

1. *Geography Explorer*   _____

2. *Raúl el ratón*   _____

3. *Las noticias con María Álvarez*   _____

4. *Amor repentino*   _____

5. *La Copa Mundial de Fútbol*   _____

6. *Jeopardy*   _____

7. *Friends*   _____

8. *Survivor*   _____

2. In small groups, decide which program should win the award *(premio)* for **"Mejor programa"** *(Best Program)* for each of the following categories.

a. First, a couple of students will volunteer to write on the board several nominees for "mejor pograma" (best program) in the various categories listed below, based on suggestions from the class.

b. Collect at least three votes from different classmates, asking them, "Para ti, ¿cuál es el mejor...?

Deporte _____ _____ _____

Programa de la vida real _____ _____ _____

Programa educativo _____ _____ _____

Dibujos animados _____ _____ _____

Comedia/Teleserie _____ _____ _____

Concurso _____ _____ _____

c. Once you've collected the votes, circle and announce the winning programs.

d. How do your outcomes compare with those of the rest of the class? Are there clear winners for each of the categories?

3. In small groups, take turns asking each other the following questions.

1. ¿Cuántos televisores tienes en casa?

2. ¿Ves la tele durante la cena?

3. ¿Te gustan los anuncios *(commercials)*?

4. ¿Prefieres ver la tele o leer un libro?

5. ¿Cuál es tu programa favorito en la tele?

¡Ojo!

As you've previously learned, certain things that you **are** in English, you **have** in Spanish. Here is a list of some common **tener** expressions.

tener ... años Tengo 23 años.	to be ... years old I am 23 years old.
tener (mucho) calor ¿Tienes mucho calor?	to be (very) hot Are you really hot?
tener (mucho) frío Ellos tienen frío.	to be (very) cold They are cold.
tener (mucha) hambre Ella tiene mucha hambre.	to be (very) hungry She's very hungry.
tener (mucha) sed Tenemos sed.	to be (very) thirsty We're thirsty.
tener (mucho) miedo (a) Tengo miedo a las arañas.	to be (very) afraid (of) I'm afraid of spiders.
tener (mucha) prisa Ella no tiene prisa.	to be in a (big) hurry She's not in a hurry.
tener (mucho) sueño El bebé tiene mucho sueño.	to be (very) sleepy The baby is very sleepy.

 ESCRIBIR

A. Complete the following sentences with the correct **tener** expression.

1. Necesito agua porque _____.

2. Miguel _____ a las serpientes.

3. ¿Cuántos _____ tu hermano? ¿13?

4. Ellos van a dormir un rato porque _____.

5. ¿Por qué corres? ¿_____?

6. ¿Dónde está la comida? ¡Yo _____!

7. Hoy _____. Necesito un abrigo *(coat)*.

8. En México, Eva _____. ¡Necesita un traje de baño!

tener
tengo
tienes
tiene
tenemos
tenéis
tienen

B. Think of characters from your favorite shows or athletes from sports teams, and make statements about them using a ***tener*** expression, based on a recent episode or game. Discuss why for each one.

1. _____ _____.
(nombre) (tener expression)

2. _____ _____.
(nombre) (tener expression)

3. _____ _____.
(nombre) (tener expression)

4. _____ _____.
(nombre) (tener expression)

C. a. Answer the following questions under the "Yo" header about your TV preferences and habits. Then, interview a classmate and record his or her answers under "compañero(a) de clase".

	Yo	Compañero(a) de clase
1. ¿Te gusta la tele? (mucho, poco, nada, etc.)		
2. ¿Cúantas horas al día ves la tele?		
3. ¿Cuál es tu programa favorito en la tele?		
4. ¿Cuál es tu programa menos favorito en la tele?		
5. ¿Con quién ves la tele típicamente?		
6. ¿Cuándo ves la tele típicamente?		

b. How do your answers compare? Discuss in class.

❖ *Lección 2: El cine* (Movies)

¿Qué tipo de película quieres ver?
What type of movie do you want to see?

Quiero ver una película...

... de acción

... de ciencia ficción

... de animación

... de terror

amorosa

¡Ojo!

Can you figure out what kinds of movies are listed here? You will see several cognates (words that have similar roots as English words). In other words, they're easy to understand!

la película...	
... de acción	action movie
... de ciencia ficción	science fiction movie
... de aventuras	adventure movie
... de animación	animated movie
... de terror	horror movie
... documental	documentary
... amorosa	romantic movie
... cómica	funny movie/comedy

PRACTICAR ———————————————————

1. In pairs, take turns asking each other the question above, and responding accordingly, naming the movie title, if you have one in mind.

2. For each of the categories listed on the previous page, share what your favorite movie is with a classmate.

Por ejemplo:
   Mi película favorita de ciencia ficción es **La guerra de las galaxias.**

   My favorite science fiction movie is Star Wars.

3. With a partner, say the following movies out loud. Can you guess what the English movie titles are? Use a dictionary, if necessary.

Los increíbles	*El mago de Oz*
El rey león	*Superhombre*
Mónstruos, S.A.	*Los juegos del hambre*
El señor de los anillos	*Hormigas*
Regreso al futuro	*La bella y la bestia*

4. Some movie titles in Spanish are quite different in meaning than the English titles. For example, the Spanish title for the movie **Home Alone**, is **Mi pobre angelito**, which literarlly means "My poor little angel".

a. Think of at least two of your favorite movies.

b. Think of a literal translation of the title in Spanish. In small groups, read the title out loud, and see if your classmates can guess what movie it is. You can also give hints in Spanish: **Es una película de animación. El tema es "dinosaurios", etc.**

c. Now, for the same movies, think of a title that is completely different than the literal translation you came up with.

Por ejemplo: Título literal: "El rey león" for Lion King, Título alternativo: "El reino de los animales" (The Animal Kingdom)

1. Película #1: _____   _____
                         (Título literal)   *(Título alternativo)*

2. Película #2: _____   _____
                         (Título literal)   *(Título alternativo)*

You have now used the two verbs "to be", **SER** and **ESTAR** in many different situations. Here's a quick review:

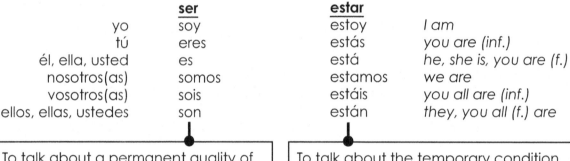

	ser	**estar**	
yo	soy	estoy	*I am*
tú	eres	estás	*you are (inf.)*
él, ella, usted	es	está	*he, she is, you are (f.)*
nosotros(as)	somos	estamos	*we are*
vosotros(as)	sois	estáis	*you all are (inf.)*
ellos, ellas, ustedes	son	están	*they, you all (f.) are*

To talk about a <u>permanent quality</u> of someone or something.

To talk about the <u>temporary condition</u> of someone or something, or <u>location</u>,

 ESCRIBIR ————————————————————

A. Complete the following statements with the verb **SER** or **ESTAR**.

1. La película _____ muy buena. Tienes que verla.

2. Los actores _____ altos y simpáticos.

3. ¿Dónde _____ el cine?

4. Nosotros _____ tristes porque no hay más entradas *(tickets)*.

5. La directora de la película _____ increíble. Quiero ver todas sus películas.

B. Fill in the following movie review chart, based on the last movie you saw. Then, share your review with your class.

Reseña de película
Movie Review

La película: _____ _____
(inglés)   (español)

El tipo de película
(Type of movie)

Es una película _____.
cómica   de animación   de acción   de aventura

El tema
(Theme)

La película es sobre _____.
un desastre   un deporte   una aventura   amor

Los personajes principales
(Main characters)

Los personajes principales son: *¿Cómo es?*
1. _____   Es _____.
2. _____   Es _____.
3. _____   Es _____.

La escena favorita
(Favorite scene)

Mi escena favorita es _____
_____
_____

Contenido
(Content)

En la película hay... (Marque todas las que apliquen)
muchas personas   pocas personas   animales
adultos   niños   súper héroes   mónstruos

Opinion final
(Final opinion)

En mi opinión, la película es...
horrible   mala   buena   fantástica

❖ *Lección 3: La vida social* (Social Life)

¿Qué usas en tu red social?
What do you use in your social network?

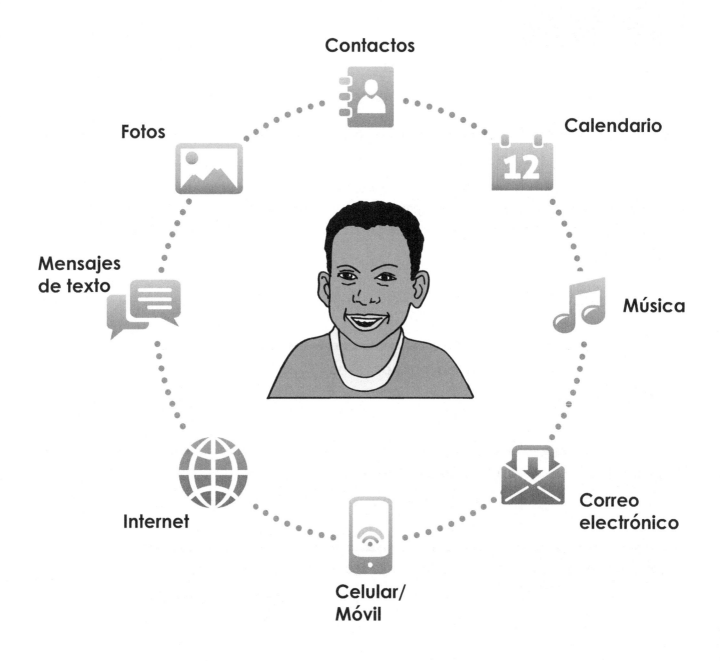

Contactos

Fotos

Calendario

Mensajes
de texto

Música

Internet

Celular/
Móvil

Correo
electrónico

el calendario	calendar	**las fotos**	photos
el celular/móvil	cell phone	**la Internet**	internet
los contactos	contacts	**el mensaje de texto**	text message
el correo electrónico	e-mail	**la música**	music

🗣 **PRACTICAR** ——————————————

1. For the following situations, discuss with a partner what you typically use in order to communicate with others or to obtain information.

Por ejemplo: ¿Qué usas para **hablar con tus abuelos**?
- Para hablar con mis abuelos, uso el móvil.

hacer planes para una fiesta   *sacar fotos*   *contar un chiste*

avisarle a un amigo que llegas tarde   *poner música a un vídeo*

encontrar un número de teléfono   *recordar el cumpleaños de alguien*

mandar la tarea a un(a) maestro(a)   *invitar a la clase a una fiesta*

_____

_____

_____

_____

_____

_____

2. As technology advances, we often stick with "older" devices with which we are familiar. For the following items, state whether you prefer the old or the new.

1. Para ver la tele, prefiero...

2. Para sacar una foto, prefiero...

3. Para escuchar música, prefiero...

4. Para hablar con mis amigos, prefiero...

5. Para ver el calendario, prefiero...

6. Para organizar mis contactos, pefiero...

7. Para mandar una carta, prefiero...

3. With a partner, create two different dialogues, by filling in the following text bubbles. Use a pencil so you can change the text if you wish.

#1

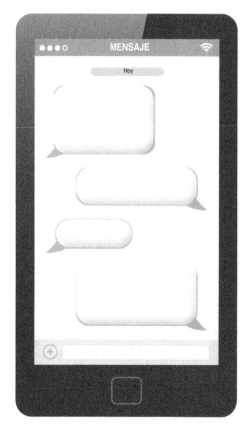

#2

¡Ojo!

Below is a quick reference for present tense conjugations:

	buscar (to search)	**creer** (to believe)	**abrir** (to open)
yo	busc**o**	cre**o**	abr**o**
tú	busc**as**	cre**es**	abr**es**
él, ella, usted	busc**a**	cre**e**	abr**e**
nosotros(as)	busc**amos**	cre**emos**	abr**imos**
vosotros(as)	busc**áis**	cre**éis**	abr**ís**
ellos, ellas, ustedes	busc**an**	cre**en**	abr**en**

The stem-changing verbs in the list below are notated in parentheses. If necessary, go to page 53 to review how they change.

abrir	to open	**encontrar** *(ue)*	to find
buscar	to search	**escribir**	to write
cargar	to charge	**escuchar**	to listen
cerrar *(ie)*	to close	**grabar**	to record
charlar	to chat	**llamar**	to call
conectar	to connect	**mandar/ enviar**	to send
descargar	to download	**publicar**	to post

 ESCRIBIR —————————————————————————

A. Complete the following sentences with the correct form of the most logical verb from your choices.

1. Yo _____ (abrir, llamar) a mis abuelos con frecuencia.

2. ¿Por qué no me _____ (mandar, cargar) tú un mensaje de texto mañana?

3. Ellos _____ (charlar, abrir) un documento sin saber lo que es. ¡Qué peligroso!

4. Nosotros no _____ (invitar, encontrar) la información que _____ (buscar, cerrar).

5. Mi madre todavía _____ (escribir, buscar) cartas *(letters)* porque es muy tradicional.

6. Ustedes _____ (publicar, cargar) sus móviles después de 2 horas. ¡No es mucho tiempo!

7. Mis amigos y yo siempre _____ (cerrar, llamar) todos los documentos en las computadoras públicas.

8. A veces yo _____ (charlar, grabar) con mis amigos sobre nada de importancia.

9. Raúl _____ (cerrar, publicar) información demasiado personal y frecuentemente.

10. Tú no _____ (escuchar, abrir) nada cuando estás en tu móvil.

B. Create your own emojis for the following *tener* expressions (see p. 98).

(see p. 98)

◯	◯	◯
Tengo calor.	**Tengo hambre.**	**Tengo miedo.**
◯	◯	◯
Tengo sueño.	**Tengo sed.**	**Tengo frío.**

C. Fill out the following social media profile page for yourself, including pictures in the spaces provided.

página social

Nombre: _____

Cumpleaños:_____
Edad: _____
Vivo en: _____
Asisto a: _____
Teléfono: _____

Amigos
☐ _____
☐ _____
☐ _____

Estado | Foto/Video

¿En qué estás pensando?

_____

Acontecimientos importantes de mi vida (con fechas)

1. _____
2. _____
3. _____

Cosas favoritas

Libro favorito: _____
Músico/Grupo favorito: _____
Canción favorita: _____
Programa de tele favorito: _____
Película favorita: _____
Deporte favorito: _____
Equipo favorito: _____
Asignatura favorita: _____

Lo que hice ayer

1. _____
2. _____
3. _____
4. _____
5. _____

❖ *Lección 4: La huella digital*
(Digital Footprint)

¿Cómo es tu huella digital?

 ¿Es útil?

¿Es positiva?

 ¿Es responsable?

¿Es segura?

¿Es verdad?

el dispositivo	device	**seguro(a)**	safe
la huella digital	digital footprint	**responsable**	responsible
positivo(a)	positive	**útil**	useful
publicar	to post	**verdad**	true

With all the perks and fun brought to us by the internet, there is also an equal amount of risk and responsibility we have to consider. The tracks we leave behind are oftentimes referred to as our "digital footprint", or ***huella digital***, in Spanish.

This personal digital history is often permanent, which is why we need to take so much care in what we post.

Nuestra huella digital se hace a través de:

• **Correo electrónico**	E-mail
• **Mensajes de texto**	Text messages
• **Comentarios en un blog, artículo, etc.**	Comments on a blog, article, etc.
• **Fotos publicadas**	Posted photos

Lo que tú dejas en Internet... ¿es útil? ¿es positivo? ¿es responsable? ¿Es seguro? ¿es verdad? **¡Ten cuidado!**

 PRACTICAR

1. In pairs, take turns asking about each other's **huella digital.**

a. ¿Cuántas horas al día pasas en un dispositivo electrónico?

b. ¿Haces muchos comentarios en textos publicados?

c. ¿Prefieres mandar correos electrónicos o mensajes de texto?

d. ¿Sacas fotos de personas sin permiso? ¿Y luego, se las mandas a otras personas?

e. ¿Hay una foto de ti en un mensaje de texto o en otro sitio?

f. ¿Qué haces cuando tienes 10 minutos libres?

2. In small groups, take turns reading the following text messages out loud. Circle the adjectives that you feel describe the message.

Me parece...

a.

> ¿Oíste que Roberto sacó una F en el examen de matemáticas? ¡Yo saqué una A!

útil	inútil
positivo	negativo
seguro	no seguro
responsalbe	irresponsable
verdad	falso

b.

> Yo puedo hacer tu aplicación. Mándame tu dirección y número de seguro social.

útil	inútil
positivo	negativo
seguro	no seguro
responsalbe	irresponsable
verdad	falso

c.

> ¡Hola amiga! Buenas suerte con tu partido de baloncesto. ¡Nos vemos pronto!

útil	inútil
positivo	negativo
seguro	no seguro
responsalbe	irresponsable
verdad	falso

d.

> Creo que todos los jugadores de fútbol son adictos a la tecnología y no duermen lo suficiente.

útil	inútil
positivo	negativo
seguro	no seguro
responsalbe	irresponsable
verdad	falso

e.

> ¿A qué hora es la fiesta de Susana? ¿Y estamos todos invitados?

útil	inútil
positivo	negativo
seguro	no seguro
responsalbe	irresponsable
verdad	falso

ESCRIBIR —————————————————————————————

A. ¿Adicto o no? Take the test below to see if you're addicted to technology.

¿Eres adicto a la tecnología?

| 0 = **Nunca/Raramente** | 1 = **De vez en cuando** | 2 = **Frecuentemente** | 3 = **Siempre** |

---

1. ¿Te sientes paralizado(a) si se te rompe tu teléfono?

| 0 | 1 | 2 | 3 |
| Nunca | | | Siempre |

2. ¿Te dicen tu familia y tus amigos que pasas mucho tiempo en Internet?

| 0 | 1 | 2 | 3 |
| Nunca | | | Siempre |

3. ¿Durante un espectáculo o evento, sacas fotos o mandas mensajes?

| 0 | 1 | 2 | 3 |
| Nunca | | | Siempre |

4. ¿Estás ansioso(a) si no puedes usar tu teléfono?

| 0 | 1 | 2 | 3 |
| Nunca | | | Siempre |

5. ¿Con qué frecuencia revisas tu correo electrónico y/o tus redes sociales?

| 0 | 1 | 2 | 3 |
| Nunca | | | Siempre |

6. ¿Perdiste una conversación una vez por estar pendiente del celular?

| 0 | 1 | 2 | 3 |
| Nunca | | | Siempre |

7. ¿Pasas más tiempo con tu teléfono que con alguién en persona ?

| 0 | 1 | 2 | 3 |
| Nunca | | | Siempre |

8. ¿Intentas reducir el tiempo que pasas en internet sin éxito?

| 0 | 1 | 2 | 3 |
| Nunca | | | Siempre |

9. Si tu teléfono se queda sin pila, ¿vuelves a casa para cargarlo?

| 0 | 1 | 2 | 3 |
| Nunca | | | Siempre |

10. ¿Usas tu teléfono mientras estudias, haces tarea o lees?

| 0 | 1 | 2 | 3 |
| Nunca | | | Siempre |

Suma los números arriba: _____   **Soy** _____.
(Add the numbers above)

0-10   **Eres sano(a).** Le das un uso apropiado a la tecnología. Pero, recuerda que hay que estar alerta ante un cambio de comportamiento.

11-20   **Eres pre-adicto(a).** Presentas los primeros síntomas de adicción y ya existen unos problemas. Intenta reducir el uso y evita la dependencia.

21-30   **Eres adicto(a).** El uso excesivo a la tecnología está causando problemas en tu vida y necesitas tomar medidas para eliminar la adicción.

❖ *Lección 5: El Repaso* *(Review)*

A. Match the Spanish words with the English counterparts.

1. mensaje	____	a.	to record
2. concurso	____	b.	news show
3. grabar	____	c.	series
4. charlar	____	d.	to send
5. película	____	e.	to charge
6. dispositivo	____	f.	science fiction
7. mandar	____	g.	digital footprint
8. noticiero	____	h.	to download
9. útil	____	i.	to post, publish
10. publicar	____	j.	message, text
11. telenovela	____	k.	to open
12. serie	____	l.	adventure
13. descargar	____	m.	movie
14. cargar	____	n.	soap opera
15. aventura	____	o.	to chat
16. huella digital	____	p.	device
17. ciencia ficción	____	q.	game show
18. abrir	____	r.	useful

B. Take turns asking your classmates the following questions.

1. ¿Estás muy presente en la red social?
2. ¿Escribes muchos mensajes?
3. ¿Escuchas audiolibros *(audio books)*?
4. ¿De qué tienes miedo?
5. ¿Tienes una huella digital?

Enfoque de Carrera

Programador
25 años
Atlanta, GA

Danny García

Laura: Hola Danny. Usted no es nativo de Atlanta, ¿verdad?

Danny: No. Soy originario de Cuba, pero llevo más de 10 años en Atlanta.

Laura: Entonces, ¿usted es *bilingüe*, no?

Danny: Sí, soy completamente bilingüe, algo muy *beneficioso* en mi trabajo.

Laura: ¿En qué sentido? ¿Me puede dar unos ejemplos?

Danny: Claro. Primero, para la *mayoría* de las *aplicaciones informáticas* que *desarrollo* tengo que crear una versión en español. Así que soy capaz de hacer las dos versiones. También, es útil para poder colaborar con amigos y familiares en Cuba que también son programadores.

Laura: ¿Qué es lo que más le gusta de su trabajo?

Danny: Me gustan los momentos de *soledad* cuando estoy *absorto* en un proyecto con una taza de café. Soy más creativo durante esos momentos.

Laura: ¿Qué es lo que menos le gusta de su trabajo?

Danny: No me gusta el aspecto fugaz de mi profesión. El tener que estar desarrollando *actualizaciones* para aplicaciones constantemente puede causar un poco de estrés.

Laura: ¿Está trabajando ahora en algún proyecto?

Danny: Sí, estoy desarrollando una aplicación para médicos en este momento, algo que les ayudará con los *diagnósticos* de pacientes *a través de* Internet.

Laura: ¿Tienes una palabra favorita en español?

Danny: Sí, sí, sin duda, mi palabra favorita en español es *cariño*.

VOCABULARIO:

bilingüe - bilingual   ***beneficioso*** - beneficial   ***mayoría*** - majority   ***soledad*** - solitude
aplicaciones informáticas - computer programs   ***desarrollar*** - to develop
absorto - absorbed   ***fugaz*** - fleeting   ***actualización*** - update   ***el tener que*** - having to
diagnósticos - diagnoses   ***a través de*** - by means of, via   ***cariño*** - love, affection

Enfoque de Carrera ◆ Discusión

A. Lee la entrevista en la página anterior en voz alta.

B. Contesta las preguntas sobre la entrevista.

1. ¿A qué se dedica Danny García? _____

2. ¿De dónde es originariamente? _____

3. ¿Dónde vive? _____

4. ¿Qué es lo que más le gusta de su trabajo? _____

5. ¿Qué es lo que menos le gusta? _____

6. ¿Habla español en su trabajo? _____

7. ¿En qué está trabajando ahora? _____

8. ¿Cuál es su palabra favorita en español? _____

◆ ◆ ◆

C. Ahora responde a las preguntas personales sobre este tema.

1. ¿Te interesan las computadoras? _____

2. ¿Qué aplicaciones usas en la computadora y/o tu teléfono? _____

3. ¿En tu opinión, ¿qué aplicación sería útil? _____

4. ¿Te gustaría ser programador(a) de aplicaciones un día? _____

5. ¿Por qué sería útil saber español en esta carrera? _____

6. ¿Cuál es tu palabra favorita en español? _____

◆ ◆ ◆

D. Comparte tus respuestas con la clase.

Glosario

SALUDOS Y DESPEDIDAS (Greetings and Farewells)   p. 2

Hola.	Hello.
Buenos días.	Good morning.
Buenas tardes.	Good afternoon.
Buenas noches.	Good night/evening.
¿Cómo te llamas?	What's your name?
Me llamo...	My name is ...
Mucho gusto.	Nice to meet you.
Igualmente.	Likewise.
¿Cómo estás?/¿Qué tal?	How are you?
(Muy) bien.	(Very) well, thanks.
Regular/Así así/Más o menos	So-so.
Mal.	Bad. / Sick.
¿Y tú?	And you?
¿De dónde eres?	Where are you from?
Soy de...	I am from...
¿Cuál es tu número de teléfono?	What is your phone number?
Hasta luego./Nos vemos.	See you later.
Adiós./Chao.	Good-bye.

LAS ASIGNATURAS (Subjects)   p. 6

el arte	art
las ciencias (naturales)	(natural) sciences
la educación física	physical education
la geografía	geography
la historia	history
la informática	computer science
la lengua extranjera	foreign language
la literatura	literature
las matemáticas	math
la música	music
la química	chemistry

LAS PROFESIONES (Professions)   p. 11

el/la abogado(a)	lawyer
el actor/la actriz	actor
el/la arqueólogo(a)	archaeologist
el/la artista	artist
el/la astronauta	astronaut
el/la bibliotecario(a)	librarian
el/la bombero(a)	firefighter
el/la carpintero(a)	carpenter
el/la científico(a)	scientist
el/la cirujano(a)	surgeon
el/la cocinero(a)	cook
el/la contable	accountant
el/la dentista	dentist
el/la diseñador(a)	designer
el/la enfermero(a)	nurse
el/la escritor(a)	writer
el/la fotógrafo(a)	photographer
el/la ingeniero(a)	engineer
el/la jardinero(a)	gardener
el/la maestro(a), profesor(a)	teacher
el/la mecánico(a)	mechanic
el/la médico(a)	doctor
el/la mesero(a), camarero(a)	waiter/waitress
el/la músico	musician

el/la peluquero(a)	hair stylist/barber
el/la piloto	pilot
el/la pintor(a)	painter
el/la plomero(a)	plumber
el/la el/la policía	police officer
el/la político	politician
el/la programador(a)	programmer
el/la secretario(a)	secretary
el/la traductor(a)	translator
el/la veterinario(a)	veterinarian

LOS QUEHACERES DOMÉSTICOS (Chores)   p. 17

barrer el suelo	to sweep the floor
cortar el pasto/el césped	to mow the lawn
fregar	to mop/to scrub/to wash
hacer la cama	to make the bed
lavar los platos	to wash the dishes
lavar la ropa	to wash the clothes
limpiar	to clean
pasar la aspiradora	to vacuum
planchar	to iron
poner la mesa	to set the table
recoger/quitar la mesa	to clear the table
regar las plantas	to water the plants
sacar la basura	to take out the garbage

LA FIESTA (Party)   p.26

abrir	to open
cantar	to sing
celebrar	to celebrate
cumplir (años)	to turn (an age)
gritar	to shout/scream
pasar(lo) bien	to have a good time
pedir un deseo	to make a wish
soplar las velas	to blow out candles
el cumpleaños	birthday
la fiesta (sorpresa)	(surprise) party
el globo	balloon
el pastel/la tarta	cake
las velas	candles
los invitados	guests
el regalo	gift

LAS EXCURSIONES (Outings)   p. 32

LA COSTA	COAST
nada	to swim
tomar el sol	to sunbathe
jugar en la playa	to play on beach
navegar	to sail
volar una cometa	to fly a kite
LAS MONTAÑAS	MOUNTAINS
acampar	to camp
caminar	to walk, hike
escalar	to climb
esquiar	to ski
hacer snowboard	to snowboard

EL CAMPO	COUNTRY
ir de pícnic	to picnic
ir de caza	to hunt
ir de pesca	to fish
ir en canoa	to canoe
montar a caballo	to horseback ride

LA CIUDAD	CITY
ir...	to go...
...al museo	...to the museum
...al teatro	...to the theater
...a un concierto	...to a concert
salir a comer/cenar	to go out to eat

LAS VACACIONES (Vacation) p. 37

el alpinismo	mountaineering
el buceo	scuba diving
el parque de atracciones	amusement park
la reunión familiar	family reunion
esquiar	to ski
sacar fotos	to take photos
viajar	to travel
las vacaciones...	
...culturales	cultural vacation
...de aventura	adventure vacation
...en crucero	cruise vacation
...en la playa	beach vacation
...en el extranjero	vacation abroad
...en casa	staycation

EL TRANSPORTE (Transportation) p. 42

el autobús	bus
el avión	airplane
el barco	ship, boat
la bici(cleta)	bicycle (bike)
el carro/el coche	car
el helicóptero	helicopter
el metro	subway
la moto(cicleta)	motorcycle
el taxi	taxi
el tren	train
caminar	to walk
manejar/conducir	to drive
ir en...	to go by...
ir a pie	to go on foot

LA ROPA (Clothing) p. 50

talla	size
rebaja	sale
apretado(a)	tight
cambiar	exchange
comprar	to buy
costar (ue)	to cost
devolver (ue)	to return
estar de moda	to be in fashion
mostrar (ue)	to show
pagar	to pay
ponerse	to put on
preferir (ie)	to prefer
probar (ue)	to try on
quedar bien/mal	to fit well/poorly

LOS DEPORTES Y EL OCIO (Sports and Liesure) p. 56

el balón	ball (big)
el bate	bat
la bici(cleta)	bike/bicycle
el casco	helmet
los esquís	skis
el guante de béisbol	baseball glove
los patines	skates
la pelota	ball (small)
la raqueta	racket
la tabla de snowboard	snowboard
el rompecabezas	puzzle
las cartas/los naipes	cards
el disco volador	frisbee
los juegos de mesa	board games
los libros de...	books
...aventura	...adventure
...suspenso	...suspense
...romance	...romance
...ciencia ficción	...science fiction
la muñeca	doll
los videojuegos	video games

LA SALUD Y LA BELLEZA (Health and Beauty) p. 62

la barbería	barber shop
el gimnasio	gym
la manicura	manicure
el maquillaje	makeup
el masaje	massage
la pedicura	pedicure
la peluquería	hair salon
las pesas	weights
la sauna	sauna
el yoga	yoga

PREPOSICIONES (Prepositions) p. 63

a la derecha de	to the right of
a la izquierda de	to the left of
al lado de	next to
debajo de	under
detrás de	behind
en	in, on
encima de	on top of
enfrente de	in front of
entre	between
sobre	over

EL HOGAR Y LA COCINA (Home and Kitchen) p. 66

LA COCINA	KITCHEN
la cafetera	coffee maker
la estufa/la cocina	stove
el horno	oven
el lavaplatos	dishwasher
la licuadora/batidora	blender, mixer
el microondas	microwave
el refrigerador/la nevera	refrigerator
el sartén	skillet
la tostadora	toaster

EL DORMITORIO	BEDROOM
la almohada	pillow
el despertador	alarm clock
las sábanas	sheets

Glosario

EL CUARTO DE BAÑO	BATHROOM
el cepillo de dientes	toothbrush
el champú	shampoo
el espejo	mirror
el jabón	soap
el papel higiénico	toilet paper
la toalla	towell

MISC.	MISC.
la aspiradora	vacuum cleaner
la escoba	broom
la lámpara	lamp
la lavadora	washing machine
la secadora	dryer
el televisor	television set

EL CICLO DE AGUA (Water Cycle) p. 75

la evaporación	evaporation
la condensación	condensation
la precipitación	precipitation
la lluvia	rain
la nieve	snow
la nube	cloud
el sol	sun
el vapor	vapor

LA CONTAMINACIÓN (Pollution) p. 78

la basura	litter/garbage
los coches/carros	cars
la contaminación	pollution
la fábrica	factory
el desagüe	drain
el humo	smoke/exhaust
el medio ambiente	environment
los productos tóxicos	toxic products
el vertido ilegal	illegal dumping

EL RECICLAJE (Recycling) p. 83

el aluminio	aluminum
la botella	bottle
el envase	jug/container
la lata	can
el papel	paper
el plástico	plastic
el reciclaje	recycling
el vidrio	glass

VIVIR VERDE (Living Green) p. 88

apagar	to turn off
echar	to throw out
plantar	to plant
reducir	to reduce
(re)usar	to (re)use
la bolsa reutilizable	reusable bag
la luz/las luces	light(s)
las pilas	batteries
los productos tóxicos	toxic products
el transporte	transportation

LA TELEVISIÓN (Television) p. 96

las comedias	comedies (sitcoms)
los concursos	game shows
los deportes	sports
los dibujos animados	cartoons
los noticieros	news shows
los programas de la vida real	reality shows
los programas educativos	educational programs
las telenovelas	soap operas
las (tele)series	TV series

EXPRESIONES CON TENER (Tener Expressions) p. 98

tener … años	to be … years old
tener (mucho) calor	to be (very) hot
tener (mucho) frío	to be (very) cold
tener (mucha) hambre	to be (very) hungry
tener (mucha) sed	to be (very) thirsty
tener (mucho) miedo (a)	to be (very) afraid (of)
tener (mucha) prisa	to be in a (big) hurry
tener (mucho) sueño	to be (very) sleepy

EL CINE (Movies) p. 100

la película...	
... de acción	action movie
... de ciencia ficción	science fiction movie
... de aventuras	adventure movie
... de animación	animated movie
... de terror	horror movie
... documental	documentary
... amorosa	romantic movie
... cómica	funny movie/comedy

LA VIDA SOCIAL (Social Life) p. 105, 107

el calendario	calendar
el célular/móvil	cell phone
los contactos	contacts
el correo electrónico	e-mail
las fotos	photos
la Internet	internet
el mensaje de texto	text message
la música	music
abrir	to open
buscar	to search
cargar	to charge
cerrar (ie)	to close
charlar	to chat
conectar	to connect
descargar	to download
encontrar (ue)	to find
escribir	to write
escuchar	to listen
grabar	to record
llamar	to call
mandar/ enviar	to send
publicar	to post

LA HUELLA DIGITAL (Digital Footprint) p. 110

el dispositivo	device
la huella digital	digital footprint
positivo(a)	positive
publicar	to post
seguro(a)	safe
responsable	responsible
útil	useful
verdad	true

ESPAÑOL ¡EN VIVO!
INSTRUCTIONAL SPANISH WORKBOOK FOR GRADES 4-8
LEVEL THREE

www.EnVivoPublications.com
360-383-7002

Made in the USA
Columbia, SC
04 August 2020